59-250-108

D1141433

Columbia University

Contributions to Education

Teachers College Series

No. 40

AMS PRESS
NEW YORK

A SPECIAL STUDY

OF

THE INCIDENCE OF RETARDATION

144818

BY

LOUIS B. BLAN, Ph.D.

TEACHERS COLLEGE, COLUMBIA UNIVERSITY
CONTRIBUTIONS TO EDUCATION, NO. 40

LC4661
B55
1972

PUBLISHED BY
Teachers College, Columbia University
NEW YORK CITY
1911

Library of Congress Cataloging in Publication Data

Blan, Louis Benjamin, 1881-
A special study of the incidence of retardation.

Reprint of the 1911 ed., issued in series: Teachers College, Columbia University. Contributions to education, no. 40.
Originally presented as the author's thesis, Columbia.
Bibliography: p.
1. Slow learning children--Case studies. I. Title. II. Series: Columbia University. Teachers College. Contributions to education, no. 40.
LC4661.B55 1972 371.92'6 79-176569
ISBN 0-404-55040-1

Reprinted by Special Arrangement with Teachers College Press, New York, New York

From the edition of 1911, New York
First AMS edition published in 1972
Manufactured in the United States

AMS PRESS, INC.
NEW YORK, N.Y. 10003

9.85

PREFACE

An attempt is made in this dissertation to measure primarily the relative frequency of non-promotion in the grades of the public school. The method of approach differs somewhat from that pursued in previous studies of the problem of retardation. The records of the local beginners or the so-called initial starters who have persisted in the present grammar grades were alone sought and from them the endeavor has been made to ascertain with some exactitude the particular grade or grades in which the pupils most frequently tend to be retarded.

Acknowledgments are due to Professor Edward L. Thorndike, of Teachers College, Commissioner David Snedden, of Massachusetts, and Professor G. D. Strayer, of Teachers College, for the kindly interest manifested and the helpful assistance tendered by them during the progress of the investigation.

The author is also indebted to the superintendents, principals, and teachers in the five city school systems visited who were especially courteous and cheerfully made every effort to assist in securing as accurate information as is possible in view of the prevailing incompleteness of the individual history or record cards.

Columbia University L.B.B.

CONTENTS

THE INCIDENCE OF RETARDATION

CHAPTER I

CRITICAL REVIEW OF THE IMPORTANT CONTRIBUTIONS TO THE STUDY OF RETARDATION

The handicap of an inadequate terminology occasions considerable ambiguity in various fields of educational endeavor. The necessity for caution in the use of " biological analogy " in one's theory of education has been pointed out by noted educational philosophers.[1] The analogous application of terms prevails quite as much in the specific fields of school study,–a tendency which here too frequently leads to difficulty.

The term "retardation" has been borrowed recently from physics, and seemingly well adapted, its use has been favored by all school-men. In defining its true meaning, however, there has arisen some difference of opinion to be explained largely in terms of relative emphasis. In one case the rate of progress, that is, the length of time it takes the pupil to do one year's work, is taken to be the proper criterion in estimating whether he is to be adjudged subnormal, normal, or supernormal. On the other hand, the age-grade standard is considered by many at once the more precise and objective measure of retardation.

Not unmindful of the fact that children vary greatly physically and mentally and hence cannot be measured at all times in terms of age-relations, the prevailing method of classification of children by grades and ages in all the progressive school systems of this country must be acknowledged as being more worth while in that it affords a better, if not the only, objective means of determining the number of backward children in our schools. The contention that retardation is not to be gleaned from the age-grade table but is to be estimated in terms of the pupil's rate of

[1] Harris, W. T., The Danger of Using Biological Analogies in Reasoning on Educational Subjects. Proceedings N. E. A., 1902:215.

speed through the grades irrespective of his age at entrance or thereafter, cannot be justified.

It has been charged by the advocates of the progress-standard that the measure of retardation in terms of a modal age group is unfair. Superintendent Greenwood, of Kansas City, rather dogmatically insists that "retardation is not a question of age without respect to progress, but it is one of time required to do a given amount of work within a specified time without regard to age." Those who voice this latter opinion do so, it would seem, more out of fear than otherwise. Since the serious import of retardation as a vital educational problem has awakened the school authorities throughout the land to investigate along these lines, some of the usual conservatives have striven to prove the alarm an exaggeration. They argue that it is sensible and intelligent for the parents to send their children to school at a late age for where such children do enter the first grade, say, at eight years of age or over, they soon make up for lost time by "skipping" classes. How, then, they ask, is it possible to gauge retardation on the basis of a hypothetical normal age for grade.

If it were definitely established that it is of little consequence when a child enters school because of this proved tendency to "skip," the progress-standard for measuring retardation certainly would hold good, but only for the lower grades, for, by the time the "over-age" entrance pupil reached the higher grades, he would be one of the normal age group himself. There is, however, little evidence other than mere opinion to prove this tendency. No adequate attempts have been made to study this important problem. Such studies on record which treat of the extent of "skipping" in our graded city schools tend to show the presence of a small percentage of these rapidly progressing pupils. How many of the "over-age" initial starters are included therein no one is in a position to say.

In a recent article published in the *Educational Review*,[1] Mr. R. P. Falkner cites from the reports of several large and small cities such statistics as he and other investigators could find which bore on the subject or revealed the amount of exceptionally rapid movement of some of the pupils through the

[1] Falkner, R. P., Retardation, its Significance and its Requirements, *Educa. R.* 1909.

grades. In Somerville, Mass., 1907, the amount of rapid progress, i.e., the promotions over more than one grade plus the promotions during the year, amounted to 1.4 per cent of all the promotions. In Springfield, Ohio, where 4,755 promotions were recorded only seven of these or not quite 0.15 per cent represented the number promoted more than one grade at the end or during the yearly term. In New York City, Mr. L. P. Ayres, of the Russell Sage Foundation, studied the records of 946 fifth grade pupils and found that 5.4 per cent of these achieved their work in less than the regularly allotted time. In one of the Philadelphia school reports, Mr. Falkner found that 2,406 pupils out of 122,644 or less than 2 per cent were thus described as incidental.

Keeping in mind, then, these small percentages of rapidly advancing pupils, it would at least seem an unwise chance for the pupil to enter the first grade at a late age and depend upon his ability solely as a result of his initial "over-ageness" to "skip" grades and make up the handicap of a year or more which he concedes his schoolmates at the very start.

Much of the dissension is attributable to the arbitrary fixing of a normal age for grade. The considerable diversity of opinion manifest demonstrates plainly the futility of defining the normal child. In some cities the so-called "theoretical age-limit" for a pupil entering the first grade is five years.[1] Others hold that a child should enter the first year of school before his seventh birthday and then if he advances regularly, he will have accomplished the eight years' course before he is fifteen years of age. Professor L. Witmer, of the University of Pennsylvania, registered the opinion,[2] when Dr. Bryan made his investigation in Camden, N. J., (1904-06) and found 72 per cent above this latter age-limit (6 years 0 months to 6 years 11 months inclusive for entrance to first grade, etc.) that only those be counted as retarded who exceeded this age-limit by one year or more. This lowered the percentages as follows: 47 per cent, one year or more over the age-limit; 26 per cent, two years or more; 13 per cent, three years or more; and 5 per cent, four years or more. Duly considering then these alarming retardation figures, Pro-

[1] In Medford, Mass., the superintendent regards five years as the proper age-standard for entrance to the first grade.

[2] Witmer, L., What is meant by Retardation? *Psy. Clinic.* Oct. 1910.

fessor Witmer tells us that it was deemed advisable to call all those pupils "pedagogically retarded" who exceeded the age-limit by two years or more and that investigators of statistics of age distribution have generally accepted this as the age-standard in their studies of the problem of retardation in other cities.

In order to properly analyze conditions in any city, statistical comparisons with other cities become imperative. Only within recent years the statistics of retardation have been published. At present they occupy a vitally important place in the annual and special reports of every efficient superintendent. Statisticians are wont to build up tables showing the relative amounts of retardation prevalent in various systems on the basis of the published percentages of "over-ageness" recorded in the respective school reports. While due precaution at times is taken to observe that in each system the same normal age-standard is assumed, nevertheless these comparisons when made simply on this basis are commonly misleading. So long as full age-grade tables are shown recording accurately the distribution of all pupils according to age, e.g., in first grade, so many 5 years 0 months to 5 years 11 months inclusive; so many 6 years 0 months to 6 years 11 months inclusive; etc., it matters little what specific theoretical age-limit is taken. The complete distributory tables furnish the only true means of comparing conditions in the schools of any given city or of city with city. The variance in interpreting just what 5 years as a normal entrance age, or 6 years, etc., really means is a real cause for many fallacious comparisons. Some understand 5 years of age to mean anywhere between 4½ and 5½ years; others regard it as 5 years 0 months to 5 years 11 months inclusive, etc. It is plain then that great care ought to be exercised in this matter of explaining the true signification of each age-heading in all age-grade tables.

Professor Witmer in the aforementioned article outlines in brief the history of the growth of the study of retardation in our schools. He asserts that the mind of the school authority was first aroused to notice the prevailing conditions of retardation among school children in the year 1895. In part this awakening is attributed to the introduction of medical inspection and to the resulting valuable medical reports tabulating the various defects of the pupils examined. Since then the literature of retardation has grown to vast proportions. Much that has been written is definite in the way of contribution towards the understanding of this serious problem of school management. In considering critically some of the publications of the leading students of retardation, the quantitative aspect of each of these studies will be treated as the fundamental concern of this dissertation. Discussions treating of the causes, and suggestions as to remedies will be omitted.

A large majority of the valuable studies of the retardation have appeared in the pages of the *Psychological Clinic,* a periodical in issue since March, 1907, edited by Professor L. Witmer, of the University of Pennsylvania. In the February number of this psychological journal, District Superintendent O. P. Cornman, of Philadelphia, collated statistics showing the amount of retardation in five selected city school systems. In the main his system of statistical tabulation demonstrated conclusively the value of the age-grade table as a standard for measuring the extent of retardation in any school and as a means for comparing the same in the school systems of various cities. Philadelphia, Boston, New York City, Camden, and Kansas City were selected for study.

Assuming 7 years to 7 years 11 months inclusive as the normal age for entrance to the first grade, Superintendent Cornman found the range of "over-ageness" to be from 51 per cent in Boston to 77.6 per cent in Kansas City.[1] From Table VI summarizing the percentages of enrollment above normal age, one notes in all five cities a progressive increase of retardation till the fifth grade and then a gradual falling off in the sixth and seventh grades and a marked drop in the eighth grade. This is especially so in Camden and in New York City. Superintendent Cornman quite correctly accounts for this on the assumption that the older children in the later grades drop out of school to go to work. Some students of retardation observing similar conditions have made the serious error of concluding that the larger retardation per cents in the lower grades proved that the earlier grades were unquestionably more difficult than the later ones. Mr. L. P. Ayres, in his investigation of the records of 20,000 New York City school pupils, is the chief offender in this re-

[1] *Psychological Clinic.* Feb. 1908: Tables I to V.

spect. He assumes the frequency of repetition in the upper grades, beginning with the sixth, is absolutely nothing and bases his estimates of retardation on this false assumption.[1]

Superintendent Cornman's study shows, then, by means of clear systematic age-distribution tables the great diversity of ages of the pupils in their respective grades and emphasizes the value of the age-grade table as unmistakable proof of the fact of retardation. That his admirable work had a considerable effect in decreasing the number of retarded pupils may at least be presumed on comparing such statistical information cited in his reports of June, 1907 and June, 1908. Whereas in the earlier year he found 12.7 per cent as being 20 or more months in one grade, in the next year there were only 6.6 per cent so retarded. It is highly probable that the marked reduction in the amount of retardation was due in large part to the mere fact that attention was called to the prevailing conditions.

In the *Psychological Clinic* issued during the month of May, 1908, Dr. R. P. Falkner, former Commissioner of Education for Porto Rico, endeavored to show some further possibilities of interpretation of the valuable statistical material gathered by Superintendent Cornman in the same five city school systems. This article is largely a special critique of method and challenges many of Superintendent Cornman's contentions. Dr. Falkner points out the significant fact that the serious effect of retardation is the shortening of the amount of education measured in time, for the few. For example, the age-grade tables of Camden, N. J., show 317 pupils in the third grade and eleven years old. In comment Dr. Falkner says that "the sad fact is not that they will be 16 years old when they reach the eighth grade but that the vast majority will never get there." Retardation means then that only the relatively few succeed in finishing the entire elementary course.

The question next under consideration is to determine to just what extent Cornman's age-grade tables are comparable. The statistical material having been gathered from annual school reports in which the grade distributions represent conditions reported at different periods throughout the year, some of the comparisons are obviously unfair. And in this connection there appears a just criticism of the methods of recording statistics

[1] Referred to again more fully on pages 12 and 13.

of enrollment as employed in these cities. In Boston, the facts are recorded at the end of the year; in Philadelphia and New York City, after the June promotions; in Camden and Kansas City, at various times during the year. Dr. Falkner discusses the three methods and declares the Boston system to be the best and the simplest. Even so, it is not considered altogether satisfactory. He suggests that the faults of this method would be obviated by recording enrollment figures on the first of October, for by that time the regular fall registration is complete and the school population has reached its maximum.

It is generally admitted by school-men and serious research students that the school reports of the majority of our cities furnish information of rather doubtful accuracy. Many of them do not show the correct age records of the pupils. Whereas accuracy is possible since the original records frequently call for age in years and date of birth, the teacher in most cases is inclined to report age in years alone irrespective of the time when the question is asked. The writer was particularly hampered while gathering material for the following quantitative study of retardation, in consequence of this neglect on the part of the teacher in the matter of securing the complete age record. It became necessary on innumerable occasions to ask the pupils individually to write out the exact date of birth, year, month, day, as well as the present age in years.

In addition, then, to this original error of the class teacher, mistakes frequently arise as a result of carelessness or even willfulness in copying off the figures of the class-room register. All these errors of transcription combine to make the final figures as reported out by the superintendent misstate the real facts. Such discrepancies as do occur when comparing the studies on the one hand of those who obtain their records from the class-room registers or individual record cards and of those research students of the official annual school reports are largely attributable to these inaccuracies in transcribing the original entries.

Noting the age-distribution tables of Superintendent Cornman, attention is called to the tremendous falling off at the age of fourteen years. Dr. Falkner commenting on the fact that at fourteen only an approximate one-half of those who are in school at twelve are still present, concludes that dropping out of school is more dependent upon age than upon the stage of grade advancement,—" a fact " which he says is " of cardinal importance in the study of retardation."

The next point of vital consequence is to consider how much there is in the prevalent contention that, were the complete statistical material at hand, the financial loss to the municipality as a result of this so-called damming of the stream of the regularly advancing pupils, would be surprisingly large. Superintendent Cornman claims that a child who takes ten years to accomplish an eight year course, costs the city 25 per cent more than one who goes through in the regular time. Whereas this may be so theoretically, the fundamental fallacy is to assume that it is actually thus in practice and to argue from it as a premise, the advisability of studying to remedy the evils of retardation. The fact must be recognized that innumerable pupils drop out of school in consequence of being held back who if regularly promoted year after year would perhaps remain throughout the entire eight year course and thus cost the city the expense of the added year or years of instruction. On the whole Professor E. L. Thorndike, of Teachers College Columbia University, estimates that " of pupils failing of promotion in the last grammar grade about one-third are eliminated before the next year's enrollment is counted; of pupils failing in the seventh grade about one-fourth; in the sixth about one-fifth; in the fifth about one-sixth."[1] Dr. Falkner in challenging Cornman's notion says " that if retardation were wholly eliminated from our schools the cost would be increased." He agrees that a wasteful expenditure of money is a result of retardation, but argues that the expenditure is wasteful largely because of its ineffectiveness. The money expended although not greater than it ordinarily would amount to yields considerably less than it would under more favorable conditions.

One of the most informational contributions to the study of retardation was made by Mr. Leonard P. Ayres, of the Russell Sage Foundation, who undertook the investigation of 20,000 pupils in fifteen schools in the Borough of Manhattan, New York City. The findings of this investigation were published in 1909 in a volume entitled, "Laggards in Our Schools." An endeavor is made to learn from the official reports of sixty-three American

[1] Thorndike, E. L. Promotion, Retardation, and Elimination. *Psy. Clinic.* Feb. 1910.

cities and from the published and unpublished school records in New York City something of the conditions and the related causes of retardation. Many important phases of the question are clearly set forth by Mr. Ayres and definite conclusions substantially correct in many cases are set down at the end of each chapter, and merit the praise due the investigator who makes definite advances toward solving so vital a problem.

Mr. Ayres' results prove beyond any question that the considerable variance in the relative amounts of retardation recorded in many of the city school reports is largely a result of the difference in method of obtaining such statistics. Tabulations must be made upon a uniform basis in order to be comparable. Assuming 6 to 8 years as the normal age for the first grade pupil; 7 to 9 years for the second grade; 8 to 10 years for the third grade; and so on, he finds that Medford, Mass., shows the least retardation of the 31 cities and the colored pupils in Memphis, Tenn., the most. Taken generally the schools of the New England States show comparatively little retardation; the schools of the Eastern and Central States record modal percentages of retardation; the schools of the Southern States, especially the colored ones, register the maximum tendency. Of course these percentages are to be considered merely as approximations as the time when the statistics were obtained varies from September, in some cases, to June in others. Again this massing of figures quite often yields results of a somewhat distorted character. To say for instance that in the 31 cities on the average 33.7 per cent of the children are above normal age for their grades means little. Far more satisfactory conclusions could be drawn were the age-grade tables of at least a few of these cities printed in full so that the student could see plainly the nature of the respective distributions. Mr. Ayres agrees that the discrepancy between the two cities, Medford, Mass., and Memphis, Tenn. (colored) which two represent the extreme cases, would not be so great were the computations made on the same basis. It is questionable if he is entirely correct in assuming that even if the data were gathered on a truly comparable basis the record of Medford would still be the best and that of Memphis, the worst.

In this connection it is well to remark that only in a few city school systems can one obtain the individual record or so-called history cards dating back more than five years.[1] In Medford, Mass., these records are obtainable and the superintendent enforces the age-standard with unusual severity; five years being taken as the normal age for a first grade pupil. In all probability this attitude explains in part the excellent showing made by this city, only 7.5 per cent of the pupils being classed as above normal age.

As a result of a laborious study of the rates of progress of pupils through the grades, Mr. Ayres has quarried out certain facts. His data show "that for every pupil making rapid progress there are from eight to ten making slow progress and for every term gained by the rapid pupils from ten to twelve are lost by the slow ones." But Mr. Ayres is not at all careful in distinguishing between the retarded pupil and the repeating pupil. For example, in his third chapter treating of the factors affecting grade distribution, Mr. Ayres discusses the factor of retardation solely on the basis of percentages of promotion. If, as he maintains, the pupils who are "over-age" at the time of entrance to the first grade make the quickest progress and by "skipping" grades soon catch up to the normal-age pupil, it follows that the percentages of repetition and retardation in the early grades would show an inverse correlation. In this case, if the complete records were obtainable the figures showing repetition could be used as a check on those of retardation directly for those pupils who are of normal age and indirectly in the case of the "over-age" pupils in question.

Quite often where there is a considerable increase in the number of pupils promoted and a corresponding decrease in the number left back to repeat the grade one or more times, the percentages above normal age may show only slight reduction. This was the case at the end of the school year 1908 in Philadelphia. Superintendent Cornman reported in June, 1907, 37.1 per cent as being above normal age and in June, 1908, 36.8 per cent, a difference of only 0.3 per cent in spite of the marked increase in percentages of promotion and decrease in percentages of "hold-overs."[2]

The writer found it quite impossible to utilize the percentages of retardation of the pupils in the eighth grades to check up

[1] In Plainfield, N. J., full history cards are kept, dating back twelve years and over.

[2] See first paragraph, page 6.

the percentages of the repeating pupils in these grades. Chart I shows the percentages of eighth grade pupils repeating one or more times during their entire school life. Chart II represents the amount of retardation in per cents of these same pupils who are now in the eighth grade.

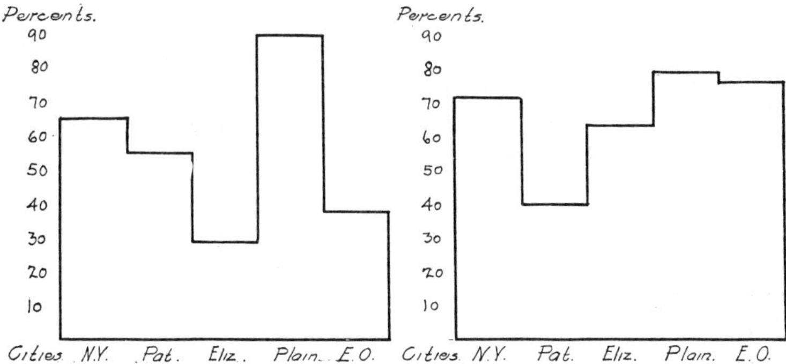

CHART 1. Percentages of eighth grade pupils repeating one or more times during entire school life

CHART 2. Percentages of retardation in the eighth grades: assuming 13 years to 13 years 11 months inclusive as the normal entrance age to the eighth grade

In New York City (one district) whereas 65 per cent of the eighth grade pupils repeated one or more times during their entire school life, 71 per cent of those in this same grade were "over-age" for grade, assuming 13 years 0 months to 13 years 11 months inclusive as the normal entrance age to the eighth grade; in Paterson 55 per cent of the eighth grade pupils repeated one or more times, and 40 per cent were found to be "over-age." In Elizabeth and East Orange the contrasts were very marked indeed. In the former the writer found only 29 per cent of repeaters as against 62 per cent of retarded pupils, and in the latter city, 38 per cent of the repeaters with 77 per cent retarded. In Plainfield the maximum of repetition was found, 90 per cent, and 78 per cent of the eighth grade pupils were above normal age for grade.[1]

The foregoing comparisons prove beyond question that it is by no means correct to use the terms repetition and retardation interchangeably. Such confusion of terms can only lead to seri-

[1] Explanation of these excessively high percentages is found on page 86.

ous error especially when the percentages of repetition are merely theoretical estimates based on the number of probable beginners, e.g., Mr. Ayres' method of determining the number of repeaters by finding what per cent the pupils in a given grade is of the probable number of beginners in the school.

But, as Professor Thorndike points out, Mr. Ayres' unpardonable error is his assumption that from the sixth grade on, the frequency of repetition is zero. His elimination and retardation figures being derived on this basis, show up much too high for grades one to six and much too low for grades six and over.

Mr. Ayres in determining the number of repeaters in the elementary grades of a given system takes the "average of the generations of the ages seven to twelve in the school membership of the system" as the number of probable beginners and uses this average as the base in such estimations. A single instance will suffice to show how far wrong Mr. Ayres' method may lead one in estimating the relative frequency of non-promotion in the grades.

According to this method the assistant superintendent of schools, Cleveland, Ohio, reckons the repeaters in the schools of his city for 1908-09 would be distributed as follows:[1]

First grade	5,260	pupils repeating
Second grade	2,216	" "
Third grade	2,243	" "
Fourth grade	1,517	" "
Fifth grade	823	" "
Sixth grade	0	" "
Seventh grade	0	" "
Eighth grade	0	" "
Total	12,059	" "

On actual investigation, however, the true figures were found to be thus distributed:

First grade	3,364	pupils repeating
Second grade	1,274	" "
Third grade	1,235	" "
Fourth grade	1,086	" "
Fifth grade	797	" "
Sixth grade	474	" "
Seventh grade	320	" "
Eighth grade	103	" "
Total	8,653	" "

[1] *Educational Review.* June, 1910.

Note, then, whereas Mr. Ayres figures that 20.2 per cent on the total registration repeated grades in the Cleveland schools during the school year, in reality the percentage of repeaters is only 14.5 per cent. His method shows an excess of 56.4 per cent on the actual number of repeaters in the first grade; 73.9 per cent more in the second; 81.6 per cent more in the third; 39.7 per cent more in the fourth; 3.3 per cent more in the fifth; and totally neglects the number of repeaters in the sixth, seventh, and eighth grades.

In the *Educational Review,* February, 1910, Professor E. L. Thorndike, of Teachers College, reviewed Mr. Ayres' book, pointing out its many valuable features. Compliment is paid the author for his having avoided certain common errors, e.g., the neglect of the inverse correlation of physical defects with age and the effect of the school entrance age upon the rate of progress therein. Many important relations, however, which could have been determined from the individual records of the New York City pupils are mentioned by the reviewer and the author is severely criticised for such omission. For example, Mr. Ayres says nothing concerning the typical rate of progress and the variations from this rate for, say 1A pupils, at the age of six, seven, etc. He neglects to ascertain the correlations between failure of promotion in a given grade and failure of promotion in subsequent grades; between failure of promotion in two or more grades and retention in other grades, e.g., comparing the sixth and seventh grades with the fourth and fifth grades with respect to the extent of non-promotion in the third grade. This sort of comparative grade study is well worth while, the resulting correlations being integral in measuring the underlying causes of failure.

The only serious attempt to gauge the comparative lengths of the different grades of the elementary school is found in a critical study made by Professor Thorndike and published in the January and February numbers, 1910, of the *Psychological Clinic,* under the caption, "Promotion, Retardation and Elimination."

Professor Thorndike carefully examined the school reports of over one hundred cities and towns and from the statements of the number of promotions by grades recorded therein, he has ascertained with a reasonable amount of accuracy the relative lengths of the various grades of city school systems in general.

Actual percentages of pupils who fail based on the grade enrollment at the end of the year are found and in order that the investigator may conveniently elicit from these figures the extent to which the grades are of unequal length, the ratios of these percentages to the average for grades two to eight are computed. It was advisable to use as the base grades two to eight rather than one to eight on account of the considerable variability among cities in the proportion of failures in the first grade.

Tables II and IV in Professor Thorndike's study show the distribution of non-promotion in grades two to eight. Table II reports on fifteen cities of which thirteen have complete data. Table IV records thirteen other cities treated in Mr. Ayres' investigation. Selecting from these two tables the cities with complete data and only those having eight yearly systems, the following two groups may be formed wherein similar tendencies prevail:

GROUP A

Proportion which the Percentage of Pupils enrolled at the End of the Year who fail of Promotion, is of the Average of such Percentages for Grade 2 to the last Grammar Grade, inclusive, in the City in Question.

GRADES	1	2	3	4	5	6	7	8
Manhattan, N. Y.	1.48	.89	.87	.98	1.09	.99	1.09	1.09
Chester, Pa......	.93	.49	.65	.85	.93	1.38	1.09	1.62
Providence, R. I..	.99	.50	.85	.78	1.21	1.35	1.49	.85
Wilkesbarre, Pa..	.45	.61	.50	.40	.71	1.11	1.41	2.22
Elgin, Ind.......	.41	.59	.75	.99	1.00	1.05	1.15	1.36
Pasadena, Cal....	1.25	.70	1.12	1.00	.88	.93	1.03	1.35
Jamestown, Va...	1.64	1.01	.93	.68	.82	.61	.97	2.00

GROUP B

(Same)

GRADES	1	2	3	4	5	6	7	8
Brooklyn, N. Y...	1.52	.91	.96	.995	1.105	1.14	1.215	.84
Fort Wayne, Ind.	2.13	.87	.94	1.05	1.22	.84	1.08	.98
Columbus, O.....	2.17	.59	.93	1.20	1.09	1.05	1.12	1.03
Philadelphia, Pa..	1.24	1.07	1.02	.96	1.19	.96	.90	.90
Chicago, Ill......	2.25	1.13	.94	.88	1.13	1.06	1.00	.81
Wheeling, W. Va.	2.08	1.25	1.13	1.46	1.42	.54	.88	.33
Springfield, O....	1.40	1.18	1.32	1.18	1.03	1.25	.81	.22
San Francisco, Cal.	.89	1.09	1.24	1.16	1.16	1.09	.81	.45
Cincinnati, O.....	1.82	1.20	1.20	1.20	.94	.88	.88	.70

Of the sixteen cities recorded above, the seven in Group A show the average length of the first four grades to be less than the average length of the last four grades; and the nine in Group

B show the reverse. The larger number in the second group is easily explained. The average weights all grades equally and as the first grade in nearly all cases is exceptionally long and the last grade in many cases rather short, several of these cities should not properly be classed in this group. The comparison would be far truer were these extreme grades eliminated. Thus comparing the averages of the lengths of the fifth, sixth, and seventh grades, one is enabled to get a more correct estimate of the relative lengths of the lower and upper grades of the city school systems in question. Groups A[1] and B[1] show then more accurately in average per cents how the three lower grades compare in length with the three higher grades.

GROUP A[1]

Average of Proportions which the Percentage of Pupils enrolled at the End of the Year who fail of Promotion in Grades 2, 3, and 4 as compared with such Averages in Grades 5, 6, and 7 is of the same Base: the Average of such Percentages for Grade 2 to last Grammar Grade inclusive.

Grades	2, 3, and 4	5, 6, and 7
Manhattan, N. Y.	.92	1.06
Chester, Pa	.66	1.13
Providence, R. I.	.71	1.02
Wilkesbarre, Pa	.50	1.08
Elgin, Ind	.78	1.07
Brooklyn, N. Y.	.96	1.15
Fort Wayne, Ind	.95	1.05
Columbus, O.	.91	1.09
Chicago, Ill	.98	1.06
Pasadena, Cal.	.94	.95

GROUP B[1]

(Same)

Grades	2, 3, and 4	5, 6, and 7
Wheeling, W. Va	1.28	.95
Springfield, O	1.23	1.03
San Francisco, Cal.	1.16	1.02
Cincinnati, O.	1.20	.90
Jamestown, Va.	.87	.80
Of equal average length in:		
Philadelphia, Pa.	1.02	1.02

If the lengths of the grades may be taken as criteria of the relative difficulty of these grades the upper grades are unquestionably more difficult than the lower. From the statistics of the entire fifteen cities gathered by Professor Thorndike, the central tendencies in the records of non-promotion figured as percentages of the June enrollment are as follows:[1]

GRADES	2	3	4	5	6	7	8
Medians......	12.25	14.00	14.75	16.00	14.25	15.00	12.50

Combining the records of these cities with those found in Mr. Ayres' report:

GRADES	1	2	3	4	5	6	7	8
Medians......	160	95	94	99.5	109	102	99.5	89

The progressive increase of non-promotion up to the sixth grade is plainly the tendency. The smaller percentages in the sixth, seventh, and eighth grades must not be taken to imply that these grades are less difficult than the earlier grades. In all probability a large number of the failing pupils in the fifth grade leave school and go to work and for those that remain, the seventh grade would seem to again function as the final selective force. Certainly if all the pupils who failed of promotion in the fifth grade remained long enough to struggle through the sixth, seventh, and eighth grades, these grades would show very much larger percentages of non-promotion. The writer found upon careful examination of the individual records of 3,865 grammar grade pupils in five city school systems that the grade distribution of non-promotion showed plainly a progressive increase of non-promotion from the first grade till the eighth grade, the seventh grade in all five cities recording the highest percentage of retention. The assumption then that very few pupils who reach the upper grades fail of promotion and repeat the work of the grade is wrong. The facts demonstrate that the retarding force in the grammar grades is certainly no less than in the primary.

It is justifiable to assume that the conditions discovered in the five cities treated in the present retardation study outline the general tendency. In this connection the reader is referred to Chapter XIX in the forthcoming 1910 report of the Commissioner of Education, written by Professor G. D. Strayer, of Teachers College, Columbia University. This chapter in so far as it touches on retardation is a summary of a statistical study soon to appear in a special bulletin issued by the Bureau of Education. It discusses the retardation and elimination of pupils as the result of

[1] *Psychological Clinic*, Jan. 1910:240.

a study of three hundred and nineteen cities of varying size in all sections of the United States. The conclusions are based on an age-grade census. The normal age is defined as six to eight for the first grade, seven to nine for the second, eight to ten for the third, and so on. Professor Strayer prefers to take the largest age group as a measure of the number entering school during the year for which the data were secured. He argues the reliability of this estimate of the entering group as opposed to the customary average of the ages seven to twelve. Wherever the actual number of beginners could be determined the latter measure has proved too small.

The tables expressing the frequency of retardation of boys and girls show the wide variability among cities. The sexes are distributed in the following manner:

QUANTITY: PER CENT OF THE TOTAL NUMBER OF BOYS   FREQUENCY: NUMBER OF CITIES

Boys Per Cent	No. of Cities		*Girls* Per Cent	No. of Cities	
			6	2	2
8	2		8	9	
10	5	16	10	7	19
12	9		12	3	
14	5		14	7	
16	1	11	16	11	28
18	5		18	10	
20	9		20	12	
22	5	22	22	20	46
24	8		24	14	
26	14		26	25	
28	17	42	28	23	67
30	11		30	19	
32	26		32	21	
34	17	66	34	18	56
36	23		36	17	
38	26		38	22	
40	16	65	40	18	49
42	23		42	9	
44	21		44	10	
46	12	51	46	3	19
48	18		48	6	
50	8		50	5	
52	5	18	52	2	10
54	5		54	3	
56	3		56	5	
58	2	11	58	7	13
60	6		60	1	

QUANTITY: PER CENT OF THE TOTAL NUMBER OF BOYS — FREQUENCY: NUMBER OF CITIES

Boys Per Cent	No. of Cities		*Girls* Per Cent	No. of Cities	
62	4	9	62	0	4
64	4		64	1	
66	1		66	3	
68	1	6	68	3	5
70	4		70	2	
72	1		72	0	
74	2	2	74	1	1

The mode ranges in the case of the boys from .32 to .42; whereas for the girls the modal range is from .26 to .36. These percentages show plainly that boys in general tend to be more retarded than girls. The theoretical age-limit allowing in each grade one year on the normal age assumed in the subjoined study accounts for the low percentages of retardation as compared with those of the five eastern school systems.

Median percentages indicating the distribution of boys and girls retarded 1 year, 2 years, 3 years, 4 years and over, again show that the boys are more frequently retarded. The cities are classified by population as follows:

POPULATION	"OVER-AGE" PUPILS								TOTAL PERCENT-AGES		"UNDER-AGE" PUPILS	
	One year		Two years		Three years		Four years and over				One year and more	
	Boys	Girls	Boys	Girls	Boys	Girls	Boys	Girls	Boys	Girls	Boys	Girls
25,000 and over (133 cities)	20	18	10	9	5	3	2	1	38	32	4	4
Less than 25,000 (186 cities)	20	18	11	8	4	3	2	1	38	36	4	5

Professor Strayer advises the separate sex classification in the study of the problem of retardation. He advocates the formation of "special classes for the bright, the slow, the backward, and the deficient." Special opportunity should be afforded those to progress in direct proportion to their ability instead of compelling the monotonous repetition of the same work over and over again.

It is significant that even assuming a rather liberal theoretical age-limit, in more than two-thirds of the cities considered, over thirty per cent of the boys are retarded. The excessive retardation in the schools of many cities throughout the country demands scientific consideration. If we would acclaim the principle of equal opportunity in our public schools, the relative amount of withdrawal, year by year and grade by grade, must be reduced. This necessitates primarily a decrease in the percentage of retarded pupils and a corresponding increase in the number accelerated.

CHAPTER II

NEW YORK CITY (One District) 1,312 CASES

The present chapter concerns the retardation of elementary school pupils only, in one school district of New York City.[1] The study was made during the months of October and November, 1909 and February, 1910. A method of investigation was used which enables one to measure the incidence of retardation, so as to estimate with some exactitude the amount of it in each grade. The cases studied are confined to pupils who began school in the kindergarten or the first grade of the school in which they now are.

The district selected is a suburban one. The six schools considered range in registry numbers from 400 to 1,500 pupils approximately. Such selection was made solely on the basis of convenience and of close personal acquaintance with the faculties of the schools.

The method employed in studying the 1,312 initial starters in this district will serve as the plan of treatment in the subsequent chapters devoted to the study of the cases recorded in the other four cities.

The Migration of Pupils

As a preliminary consideration it is worth while to note the following tabulated comparison by grades of the net results of the effect of the migratory tendency plus the tendency to enter the grades beyond the first.

A rather poor statistical measure, yet interesting in this case, is the range in per cent of the effect of the migratory tendency in the various sections of a school district. It is seen in Table I to be from 22 per cent to 62 per cent, i.e., whereas in School F the pupils who are now in the grammar grades and who entered the kindergarten or the 1 A grade represent about one-fifth of the present total register in these grades, in School A there are,

[1] This chapter was published as a special article in the *Educational Review*, June, 1910. Some changes have been made in the text. Table 6 has been added and sex distributions are shown.

subject to the same conditioning factor, more than three times as many. The 78 per cent in the one case or the 38 per cent in the other would represent the migration from other schools plus the number of those who were admitted as absolutely new pupils in or beyond the second grade. As a matter of fact the number of such absolutely new admissions is unquestionably

TABLE 1

PER CENTS OF INITIAL STARTERS [1]

Schools	A	B	C	D	E	F	Aver.
Grades	per cent	per cent	per cent	per cent	per cent	per cent	per cent
8B	60	26	60	44	45	27	43.7
8A	57	34	45	30	50	6	37.0
7B	62	32	46	38	36	17	38.5
7A	56	17	29	31	42	17	32.0
6B	64	44	43	19	58	40	44.7
6A	51	46	71	25	43	11	41.2
5B	59	53	71	24	49	17	45.5
5A	72	58	48	66	51	17	52.0
4B	81	100	56	45	46	40	61.3
4A	58	91	60	50	63	26	58.0
Average	62	50	53	37	48	22	45.3

[1] The quotients obtained by dividing the numbers of pupils in each grade, who entered the school in which they are at present enrolled in either the 1A grade or in the kindergarten, by the present total register of the grade in which they now are, are changed to per cents.

so small that it is scarcely worth considering. Taken generally the net results obtained by subtracting the per cents given from 100 per cent show quite accurately the migratory tendency prevalent in the district studied.

Considering the 7 A grades in aggregate one notes that the minimum of 32 per cent, and in all the 4 B grades the maximum of 61.3 per cent show similarly the wide range in grade distribution of those who originally entered the lowest grade of school. Or more generally in grades 6 A and up through 8 B, on the average 60 per cent of the registered pupils have been received mostly by transfer from other schools to, or have been admitted as new pupils in grades beyond, the 1 A grade. On the other hand in grades 5 B and down through 4 A there is a decrease of 25 per cent on that rate, showing 45 per cent as not having entered the initial grade of the school in which they now attend.

The Age-Grade Relations of the 1,312 Initial Starters

The actual numbers of pupils in the grades of the six schools are shown, segregated according to ages, in Table 2. The age of each individual is given in years only and represents the entrance age to the present grade. In the last column of Table 2 the numbers of retarded pupils are changed to per cents.

TABLE 2

Six Schools. Age Distribution. Aggregate 1,312 Cases

Grade	7 or less	8	9	10	11	12	13	14	15	16	17 or more	Total	Above Normal Age	
													No.	Per cent
8B							28	27	19	7	2	83	55	66.3
8A						2	13	24	23	3		65	50	76.9
7B					1	14	33	30	10	8		96	81	84.4
7A				1	4	18	33	18	15	4	2	95	72	75.8
6B					20	40	39	29	7	3		138	118	85.5
6A				2	45	41	30	17	9	1		145	98	67.6
5B			1	24	50	47	23	13	6			164	139	84.8
5A			1	42	48	36	13	7	4	1		152	109	71.7
4B			26	61	47	34	13	7	2			190	164	86.3
4A	1	16	48	55	35	13	11	5				184	119	64.7
								Total..........				1,312	Cases	

Assuming 9 years to 9 years 11 months inclusive as the normal entrance age in grade 4 A, had no pupils been delayed in entering school or held back thereafter in the six schools considered, in general it may be said that 66.3 per cent of those in 8 B who entered their respective schools in the first grade, are "over-age"; 76.9 per cent in 8 A; 84.4 per cent in 7 B, etc., to 64.7 per cent in 4 A. Taking 6 years to 6 years 11 months inclusive as the normal entrance age to grade 1 A, 7 years to 7 years 11 months inclusive to grade 2 A, 8 years to 8 years 11 months inclusive to grade 3 A, 9 years to 9 years 11 months inclusive to grade 4 A, etc., the writer is following the usual custom. In reality the modal entrance age in the schools of the particular district studied, as shown by Table 2, is almost seven years, probably 6 years 10 months or thereabouts. Percentages of "over-ageness" as stated in the last column of Table 2 are therefore too high. Taking 10 years to 10 years 11 months inclusive as the normal age of a pupil entering the fourth grade, these percentages for 8 B through 4 A would reduce to 33.7, 40.0, 50.0, 41.1, 56.5, 39.3, 54.3, 40.1, 56.8, 34.8, respectively.

The accompanying graph illustrates in per cents the modes, maxima and minima, of retardation by grades in the various schools:

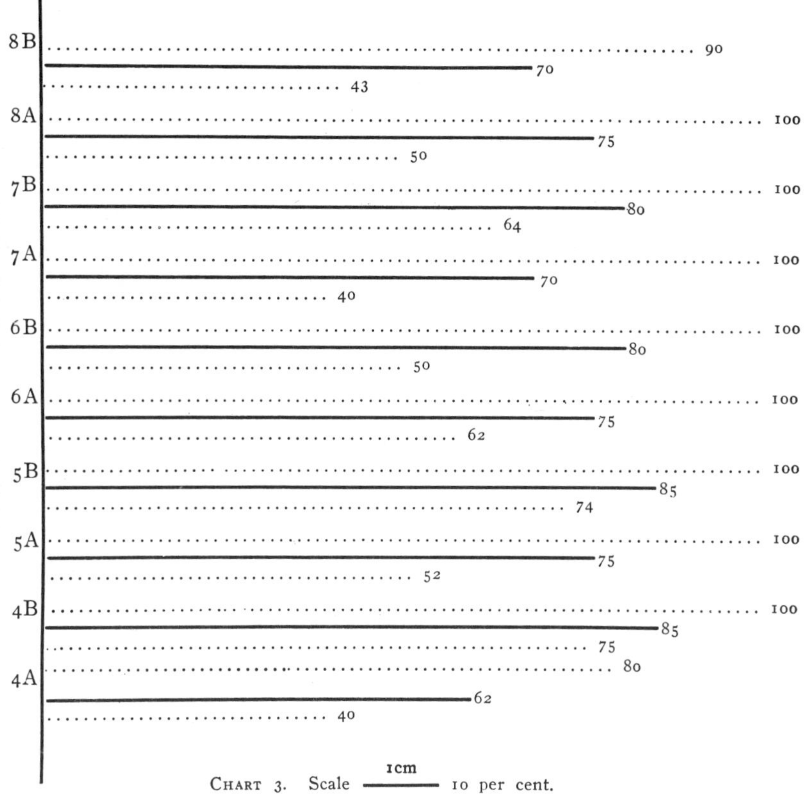

CHART 3. Scale ——— 10 per cent.

Table 3 shows in full the approximate modes by grades, deviations from these modes and average deviations.

TABLE 3

RETARDATION IN PER CENTS. BASED ON ENTRANCE AGE TO PRESENT GRADE

Schools	A	B	C	D	E	F	Approx. Mode	Deviations from Mode						Aver. Dev.
								A	B	C	D	E	F	
Grades	per cent	per cent	per cent	per cent	per cent	per cent	per cent	per cent	per cent	per cent	per cent	per cent	per cent	per cent
8B	73	88	43	73	90	50	70	+3	+18	—27	+3	+20	—20	15.2
8A	71	98	77	50	73	100	75	+4	+23	+2	—25	—2	+25	13.5
7B	92	96	74	64	100	67	80	+12	+16	—6	—16	+20	—13	13.8
7A	77	67	80	100	69	40	70	+7	—3	+10	+30	—1	—30	13.5
6B	86	97	81	100	78	50	80	+6	+17	+1	+20	—2	—30	12.7
6A	66	68	62	75	74	100	75	—9	—7	—13	0	—1	+25	9.2
5B	93	88	74	88	83	100	85	+8	+3	—11	+3	—2	+15	7.0
5A	67	89	52	79	75	100	75	—8	+14	—23	+4	0	+25	12.3
4B	90	83	76	100	95	75	85	+5	—2	—9	+15	+10	—10	8.5
4A	66	80	54	45	70	40	60	+6	+20	—6	—15	+10	—20	12.8

The sex distributions of retarded pupils in the grades 4 A through 8 B are shown in the following table and comparative charts. The plain type in each square numbers the boys graded according to entrance age to present class; the numbers of girls are printed in italics in the upper part of these same squares.

The last column in Table 4 indicates the ratios in per cents of the boys above normal age to the total number of boys in their respective classes and the figure above in each case indicates the ratio in per cent of the "over-age" girls to the total number of girls. A statement then such as the following may be made: Whereas 65.1 per cent of the total number of male initial starters now in grade 8 B are above the assumed normal age 13 years to 13 years 11 months inclusive, 67.5 per cent of the total number of female initial starters now in this same class are thus graded "over-age." However, in only three grades, 8 B, 6 A, and 5 B, are there larger percentages of retarded girls than boys. Charts 4 a and 4 b illustrate plainly the tendency in this New York City district. The median for the ten grades in the case of the 665 boys is 79.0 per cent; and for the 647 girls it is 75.0 per cent.

TABLE 4

SIX SCHOOLS. AGE-GRADE TABLE SHOWING SEX DISTRIBUTION

Boys in plain type. Girls in italics.

Grades	7 or less	8	9	10	11	12	13	14	15	16	17 or more	Total	Above Normal Age No.	Above Normal Age Per cent
8B							*13* 15	*12* 15	*10* 9	*3* 4	*2* 0	*40* 43	*27* 28	*67.5* 65.1
8A						*0* 2	*6* 7	*10* 14	*6* 17	*2* 1		*24* 41	*18* 32	*75.0* 78.0
7B					*1* 0	*8* 6	*16* 17	*14* 16	*3* 7	*5* 3		*47* 49	*38* 43	*80.9* 87.8
7A				*1* 1	*2* 2	*11* 7	*17* 16	*10* 8	*7* 8	*3* 1	*2* 0	*52* 43	*39* 33	*75.0* 76.7
6B					*10* 10	*16* 24	*18* 21	*14* 15	*4* 3	*3* 0		*65* 73	*55* 63	*84.6* 86.3
6A				*0* 2	*19* 26	*25* 16	*13* 17	*9* 8	*3* 6	*1* 0		*70* 75	*51* 47	*72.9* 62.7
5B			*1* 0	*7* 17	*26* 24	*26* 21	*11* 12	*5* 8	*3* 3			*79* 85	*71* 68	*89.9* 80.0
5A			*0* 1	*32* 10	*21* 27	*22* 14	*5* 8	*6* 1	*1* 3	*0* 1		*87* 65	*55* 54	*63.2* 83.1
4B			*18* 8	*30* 31	*20* 27	*17* 17	*6* 7	*2* 5	*1* 1			*94* 96	*76* 88	*80.8* 91.7
4A	*0* 1	*9* 7	*23* 25	*28* 27	*13* 22	*7* 6	*6* 5	*3* 2				*89* 95	*57* 62	*64.0* 65.3
											Total......	*647* 665	Girls Boys	

(Charts 4 a and 4 b referring to Table 4 are found on page 30.)

It has been suggested that it is unfair to assume that six years is the average entrance age of a pupil admitted to the 1 A grade in the schools of this city. Table 5 is a simple statement of the ages at entrance to 1 A grade of the 1,312 children treated in this chapter.

Reading from Table 5, one notes that of the 373 initial starters in School A, 46 entered grade 1 A at the age of five or less; 137, at the age of six; 119, at seven; and 71, at eight years or more. This means that about one half of these children were "over-age" at the time of their entrance to the first grade.

TABLE 5

AGE DISTRIBUTION OF 1,312 PUPILS AT TIME OF ENTRANCE TO 1 A GRADE

Schools	5 or less	6	7	8 or more	Total	Above Normal Age	
						No.	Per cent
A	46	137	119	71	373	190	50.9
B	31	109	81	58	279	139	49.8
C	34	162	90	34	320	124	38.8
D	11	40	53	13	117	66	56.4
E	17	74	55	41	187	96	51.3
F	10	12	9	5	36	14	38.9
Total	149	534	407	222	1,312	629	47.9

For the six schools, about 48 per cent of the 1,312 pupils treated were over six years of age (i.e., 6 years 0 months to 6 years 11 months inclusive) when they were admitted to grade 1 A. The large numbers in the seven-year and eight-year columns are, perhaps, to be accounted for by the fact that prior to October 1, 1909 the compulsory attendance age in the schools of this city ranged from eight to sixteen. At present the amended Compulsory Education Law says, in part, that "every child between seven and sixteen years of age, in proper physical and mental condition to attend school, shall regularly attend upon instruction during the compulsory school year."

In order to learn more in detail concerning the age records of the 1,312 initial starters as furnished in Table 6, the following table was constructed to show how old these pupils were when they entered the 1 A class, distributed according to present grade.

The extreme column on the right in Table 6 tells us that 48.2 per cent of the present 8 B pupils were "over-age" at the time

TABLE 6

AGE-GRADE DISTRIBUTION OF 1,312 PUPILS AT TIME OF ENTRANCE TO 1A GRADE

Ages	Five Years or Less						Six Years						Seven Years						Eight Years or More						Total	"Over-Age"	
Schools	A	B	C	D	E	F	A	B	C	D	E	F	A	B	C	D	E	F	A	B	C	D	E	F	Cases	No.	Per cent
Grades 8B	2	1	2	1	0	0	8	2	16	3	6	2	4	2	13	4	2	2	1	3	4	3	2	0	83	40	48.2
8A	1	1	2	1	1	1	9	8	6	1	4	0	5	5	4	3	5	0	2	3	1	1	1	0	65	30	46.2
7B	6	4	3	0	0	1	6	4	9	3	3	0	3	9	10	7	3	1	9	6	5	1	2	1	96	57	59.4
7A	6	3	3	2	1	1	7	4	9	1	4	3	8	3	9	5	2	1	10	2	4	1	6	0	95	51	53.7
6B	3	1	2	0	2	2	12	12	30	2	6	2	15	11	8	4	6	0	6	8	2	0	4	0	138	64	46.4
6A	2	1	2	1	1	1	18	21	22	7	9	1	8	12	11	4	5	0	7	4	4	0	4	0	145	59	40.7
5B	2	2	10	1	1	1	20	16	18	3	11	1	17	9	11	3	11	0	7	6	7	1	6	0	164	78	47.6
5A	11	2	2	3	1	1	16	8	12	4	4	0	21	10	9	9	7	0	10	8	2	3	8	1	152	88	57.9
4B	12	10	3	1	5	2	21	15	19	7	8	1	26	12	8	2	4	3	11	10	3	3	2	2	190	86	45.3
4A	1	6	5	1	5	0	20	19	21	9	19	2	12	8	7	12	10	2	8	8	2	0	6	1	184	76	41.3
Total	46	31	34	11	17	10	137	109	162	40	74	12	119	81	90	53	55	9	71	58	34	13	41	5	1,312	629	47.9

of their entrance to the 1 A grade; 46.2 per cent in 8 A; 59.4 per cent in 7 B, etc., to 41.3 per cent in 4 A. In all the grades from 4 A to 8 B inclusive, the percentages range from 40.7 to 59.4. The fourth and sixth grades show minimum percentages of initial "over-ageness"; the fifth and seventh, maximum percentages. Referring to Table 2 one notes that the present percentages of "over-ageness" in the fifth and seventh grades are larger than those in the other grades. The natural tendency is to conclude that a large proportion of such "over-ageness" is the result of original "over-ageness" at the time of school entrance as recorded in Table 6. For example, one is inclined to say that out of the 66.3 per cent of "over-age" pupils now in 8 B, 48.2 per cent were "over-age" at the time of entrance to the 1 A grade. This is by no means correct for the forty pupils in the one case do not of necessity refer to the same 40 individuals out of 55 who are now graded as "over-age" in 8 B. Whereas the same groups are referred to, it was found impossible under the present circumstances to handle the individual records of these pupils so as to afford an explanation of the exact amount of present "over-ageness" due to initial "over-ageness." All that one is justly entitled to say concerning these percentages of pupils above normal age as recorded in Tables 2 and 6 is that these percentages in both cases are relatively high. It is probable then that a large proportion of these present "over-age" pupils were "over-age" at the time of their entrance to the 1 A grade, in so far as there are at present in the 8 B grade only 83 initial starters of which 40 were above normal age when they began school and 55 are "over-age" now.

Table 7 shows the initial age-grade records of the 1,312 cases distributed according to sex, and the appended charts illustrate graphically the "over-age" boys at the time of their entrance to the 1 A grade as compared with the "over-age" girls.

From Table 7, of the boys who remain through the fourth, fifth, sixth, seventh, and eighth grades about 50 per cent were over 6 years 11 months when they entered the 1 A grade; of the girls, about 46 per cent. In this district then the boys remaining in all the grammar grades who entered the first class of the school in which they now are, show larger percentages

Age-Grade Sex Distribution of 1,312 Pupils at Time of Entrance to 1A Grade

Boys in plain type. Girls in italics.

Ages	Five Years or Less						Six Years						Seven Years						Eight Years or More						Total Cases	"Over-Age"	
Schools	A	B	C	D	E	F	A	B	C	D	E	F	A	B	C	D	E	F	A	B	C	D	E	F		No.	Per cent
Grades 8B	*1*	*1*	*1*	*1*	*0*	*0*	*6*	*1*	*7*	*2*	*4*	*0*	*3*	*0*	*5*	*2*	*2*	*0*	*0*	*2*	*1*	*0*	*1*	*0*	*40*	*16*	*40.0*
	1	0	1	0	0	0	2	0	9	1	2	2	1	2	8	2	0	2	1	1	3	3	1	0	43	24	55.8
8A	*0*	*0*	*1*	*0*	*0*	*1*	*2*	*4*	*3*	*1*	*1*	*0*	*1*	*2*	*2*	*2*	*1*	*0*	*1*	*2*	*0*	*0*	*0*	*0*	*24*	*11*	*45.8*
	1	1	1	1	1	0	7	4	3	0	3	0	4	3	2	1	4	0	1	1	1	1	1	0	41	19	46.3
7B	*4*	*2*	*1*	*0*	*0*	*0*	*5*	*1*	*3*	*2*	*1*	*0*	*2*	*1*	*4*	*6*	*1*	*1*	*6*	*3*	*1*	*1*	*1*	*1*	*47*	*28*	*59.6*
	2	2	2	0	0	1	1	3	6	1	2	0	1	8	6	1	2	0	3	3	4	0	1	0	49	29	59.2
7A	*3*	*2*	*2*	*1*	*1*	*0*	*5*	*3*	*7*	*1*	*3*	*1*	*1*	*2*	*4*	*2*	*2*	*0*	*6*	*1*	*1*	*0*	*4*	*0*	*52*	*23*	*44.2*
	3	1	1	1	0	1	2	1	2	0	1	2	7	1	5	3	0	1	4	1	3	1	2	0	43	28	65.1
6B	*2*	*0*	*1*	*0*	*1*	*1*	*6*	*8*	*15*	*1*	*2*	*1*	*7*	*4*	*3*	*3*	*2*	*0*	*3*	*4*	*0*	*0*	*1*	*0*	*65*	*27*	*41.5*
	1	1	1	0	1	1	6	4	15	1	4	1	8	7	5	1	4	0	3	4	2	0	3	0	73	37	50.7
6A	*1*	*0*	*1*	*0*	*0*	*1*	*8*	*11*	*12*	*4*	*4*	*0*	*4*	*5*	*5*	*1*	*3*	*0*	*4*	*3*	*2*	*0*	*1*	*0*	*70*	*28*	*40.0*
	1	1	1	1	1	0	10	10	10	3	5	1	4	7	6	3	2	0	3	1	2	0	3	0	75	31	41.3
5B	*1*	*1*	*6*	*0*	*0*	*1*	*7*	*10*	*10*	*1*	*6*	*0*	*8*	*4*	*4*	*1*	*7*	*0*	*3*	*3*	*4*	*0*	*2*	*0*	*79*	*36*	*45.6*
	1	1	4	1	1	0	13	6	8	2	5	1	9	5	7	2	4	0	4	3	3	1	4	0	85	42	49.4
5A	*5*	*1*	*1*	*2*	*1*	*0*	*8*	*6*	*10*	*2*	*3*	*0*	*11*	*6*	*7*	*3*	*4*	*0*	*6*	*5*	*1*	*1*	*4*	*0*	*87*	*48*	*55.2*
	6	1	1	1	0	1	8	2	2	2	1	0	10	4	2	6	3	0	4	3	1	2	4	1	65	40	61.5
4B	*5*	*5*	*2*	*1*	*2*	*1*	*10*	*7*	*9*	*5*	*5*	*1*	*12*	*5*	*3*	*1*	*2*	*2*	*6*	*4*	*2*	*1*	*1*	*2*	*94*	*41*	*43.6*
	7	5	1	0	3	1	11	8	10	2	3	0	14	7	5	1	2	1	5	6	1	2	1	0	96	45	46.9
4A	*0*	*4*	*0*	*0*	*1*	*0*	*12*	*10*	*11*	*3*	*8*	*1*	*7*	*4*	*6*	*3*	*5*	*1*	*4*	*5*	*1*	*0*	*3*	*0*	*89*	*39*	*43.8*
	1	2	5	1	4	0	8	9	10	6	11	1	5	4	1	9	5	1	4	3	1	0	3	1	95	37	38.9
Total	*22*	*16*	*16*	*5*	*6*	*5*	*69*	*61*	*87*	*22*	*37*	*4*	*56*	*33*	*43*	*24*	*29*	*4*	*39*	*32*	*13*	*3*	*18*	*3*	*647*	*297*	*45.9*
	24	15	18	6	11	5	68	48	75	18	37	8	63	48	47	29	26	5	32	26	21	10	23	2	665	332	49.9

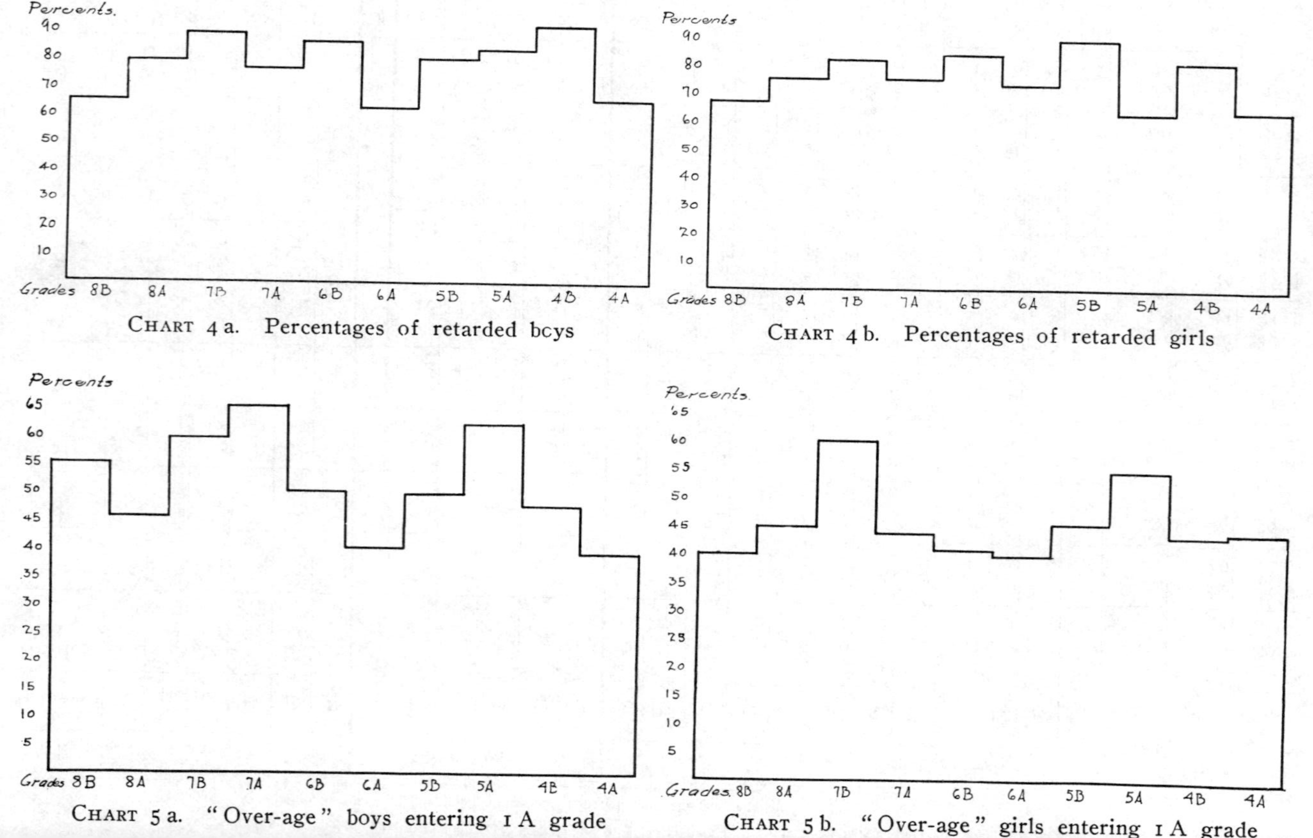

CHART 4 a. Percentages of retarded boys

CHART 4 b. Percentages of retarded girls

CHART 5 a. "Over-age" boys entering 1 A grade

CHART 5 b. "Over-age" girls entering 1 A grade

of initial "over-ageness" than the girls. At the same time one notes in Table 4 that these boys now in the grammar grades tend to be more retarded than the girls. In the eighth and seventh grades, the median percentage for "over-age" boys (Table 4) is 77.4; for "over-age" girls it is 75.0; whereas from Table 7 the median percentages of initial "over-ageness" of boys and girls for these same grades are 58.1 and 44.6 respectively. Other things being equal these figures would indicate the probability that the selected boys who reach the high grades and are retarded, are so more as a result of their initial "over-ageness" than is the case with the retarded girls.

Charts 5 a and 5 b show clearly that in the matter of "over-ageness" at the time of school entrance boys are considerably more variable per grade than girls.

The Incidence of Retardation

The second part of this chapter is devoted to the measurement of the relative frequency of non-promotion in the different grades. Each pupil was asked to state in what grade or grades he had been kept back for a second term. In the event of the pupil's inability to remember accurately, a note was made of such inability and recourse was had to the record card filed in the office of the principal. Such action was necessary in 32 out of 1,312 cases and the writer was particularly fortunate in obtaining full records of same; for it was noted that in the majority of cases the record cards of the upper grade pupils did not show in full their history since their entrance into grade 1 A. The records usually read back only as far as 1904. This explains why it became necessary to visit each and every class in grades 4 A through 8 B in the six schools in order to obtain direct from the pupils the information sought. This information was checked up by the records when possible.

In the first place an endeavor was made to ascertain the frequency of non-promotion of those pupils now in the grammar grades including 4 A and 4 B.

The figures in Table 8 a show how many pupils of the initial starters who had reached any given grade from 4 A on, in the six schools, had been "held back" once, twice, three times, etc. Converting these figures to per cents for purposes of comparison, we have Table 8 b. These figures do some of the pupils an injustice in that no allowance was made in the case of those pupils who failed in a given grade but "skipped" a grade either previously or thereafter.

TABLE 8a

Six Schools. Aggregate 1,312 Cases

Left Back	4A	4B	5A	5B	6A	6B	7A	7B	8A	8B
None	78	68	42	67	45	41	30	40	17	36
One	64	53	54	41	36	40	23	27	23	20
Two	25	35	36	38	42	39	26	24	17	21
Three	9	20	10	15	15	13	8	5	7	2
Four	4	7	6	3	7	5	5	0	1	3
Five or More	4	7	4	0	0	0	3	0	0	1
Total Left Back	106	122	110	97	100	97	65	56	48	47
Total Cases	184	190	152	164	145	138	95	96	65	83

TABLE 8b

Same Converted to Per Cent Equivalents

Left Back	4A	4B	5A	5B	6A	6B	7A	7B	8A	8B
	per cent	per cent	per cent	per cent	per cent	per cent	per cent	per cent	per cent	per cent
None	42	36	28	41	31	30	32	42	26	43
One	35	28	36	25	25	29	24	28	35	24
Two	14	18	24	23	29	28	27	25	26	25
Three	5	11	7	9	10	9	8	5	11	2
Four	2	4	4	2	5	4	5	0	2	4
Five or More	2	4	3	0	0	0	3	0	0	1
Total Left Back	58	65	74	59	69	70	67	58	74	56

The opinion has been expressed by many of the teachers and principals questioned at the time of the investigation that the so-called " average " pupil, mentally, does reach the 8 B grade but is left back at least twice during his or her school life. The use of the expression "average" pupil is confusing, to say the least. Whether or not those who enter 1 A and pass through 8 B in the same school are of average ability, the fact is that almost one half of these pupils are never left back at all; one fourth, once; one fourth, twice; 2 per cent, three times; 4 per cent, four times; and 1 per cent, five times or more. The median evidently would be somewhere in the "one-time" group.

These same data are distributed according to sex in the following tables. The charts compare eighth grade boys and girls with respect to promotion and repetition during their entire school life.

TABLE 9a

PUPILS REPEATING AND NON-REPEATING DURING ENTIRE SCHOOL LIFE

Boys in plain type. Girls in italics.

Left Back	4A	4B	5A	5B	6A	6B	7A	7B	8A	8B
None	*38* 40	*36* 33	*31* 11	*35* 32	*21* 24	*17* 24	*19* 11	*18* 22	*7* 10	*15* 21
One	*33* 31	*28* 25	*29* 25	*21* 20	*18* 18	*17* 23	*10* 13	*13* 14	*12* 11	*12* 8
Two	*11* 14	*19* 16	*17* 19	*18* 20	*23* 19	*22* 17	*15* 11	*13* 11	*4* 13	*11* 10
Three	*3* 6	*7* 13	*5* 5	*5* 10	*6* 9	*5* 8	*5* 3	*3* 2	*1* 6	*1* 1
Four	*1* 3	*4* 3	*4* 2	*0* 3	*2* 5	*4* 1	*2* 3	*0* 0	*0* 1	*1* 2
Five or More	*3* 1	*1* 6	*1* 3	*0* 0	*0* 0	*0* 0	*1* 2	*0* 0	*0* 0	*0* 1
Total Left Back	*51* 55	*59* 63	*56* 54	*44* 53	*49* 51	*48* 49	*33* 32	*29* 27	*17* 31	*25* 22
Total Cases	*89* 95	*94* 96	*87* 65	*79* 85	*70* 75	*65* 73	*52* 43	*47* 49	*24* 41	*40* 43

TABLE 9b

SAME CONVERTED TO PER CENT EQUIVALENTS

Boys in plain type. Girls in italics.

Left Back	4A	4B	5A	5B	6A	6B	7A	7B	8A	8B	Average[1] 8A and 8B
	per cent	per cent	per cent	per cent	per cent	per cent	per cent	per cent	per cent	per cent	per cent
None	*42.7* 42.1	*37.2* 34.4	*35.6* 16.9	*44.3* 37.6	*30.0* 32.0	*26.2* 32.9	*36.5* 25.6	*38.3* 46.9	*29.2* 24.4	*37.5* 48.8	*34.4* 36.9
One	*37.2* 32.6	*29.8* 26.0	*33.3* 38.5	*26.6* 23.5	*25.7* 24.0	*26.2* 31.5	*19.2* 30.2	*27.7* 28.6	*50.0* 26.8	*30.0* 18.6	*37.5* 22.6
Two	*12.4* 14.7	*20.2* 16.7	*19.5* 29.2	*22.8* 23.5	*32.9* 25.3	*33.8* 23.3	*28.8* 25.6	*27.7* 22.4	*16.7* 31.7	*27.5* 23.3	*23.4* 27.4
Three	*3.4* 6.3	*7.4* 13.5	*5.7* 7.7	*6.3* 11.8	*8.6* 12.0	*7.7* 11.0	*9.6* 7.0	*6.4* 4.1	*4.2* 14.6	2.5 2.3	*3.1* 8.3
Four	*1.1* 3.2	*4.3* 3.1	*4.6* 3.1	*0.0* 3.5	*2.9* 6.7	*6.2* 1.4	*3.8* 7.0	*0.0* 0.0	*0.0* 2.4	2.5 4.7	*1.6* 3.6
Five or More	*3.4* 1.1	*1.1* 6.3	*1.1* 4.6	*0.0* 0.0	*0.0* 0.0	*0.0* 0.0	*1.9* 4.7	*0.0* 0.0	*0.0* 0.0	*0.0* 2.3	*0.0* 1.2
Total Left Back	*56.2* 57.9	*62.8* 65.6	*64.4* 83.1	*55.7* 62.4	*70.0* 68.0	*73.8* 67.1	*63.5* 74.4	*61.7* 55.1	*70.8* 75.6	*62.5* 51.2	*65.6* 63.1

[1]These percentages are derived from the 8A and 8B columns of Table 9a. Use sum of 41 + 43 = 84 as base for Boys ; 24 + 40 = 64 as base for Girls.

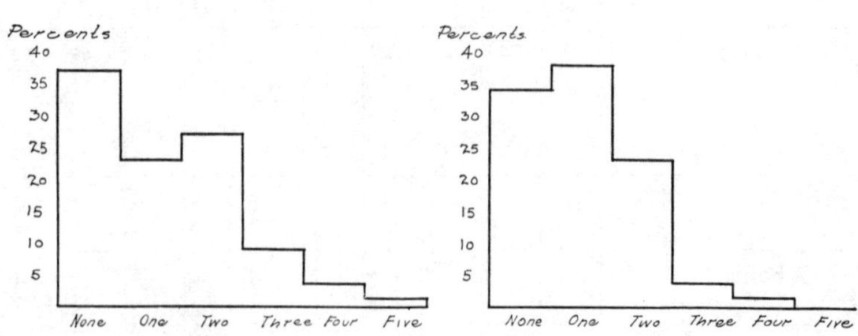

CHART 6 a. Eighth grade boys. Repeaters and non-repeaters during school life

CHART 6 b. Eighth grade girls. Repeaters and non-repeaters during school life

The top row of Table 9 b records, in grades 4 A through 5 B as compared with grades 6 A through 8 B, the girls promoted in larger numbers than the boys. The larger percentage of regularly promoted boys then considering only those who reach the highest grades in this school district would indicate that these boys are brighter than their girl classmates. On the other hand, whereas larger percentages of eighth grade girls left back once during their entire school life are recorded, the percentages of boys left back twice, three, four, and five or more times by far exceed those of the girls.

Charts 6 a and 6 b again show the boys who are successful in their elementary school work to be more variable than the girls in the matter of promotion and non-promotion. It would seem in this district at any rate that the boys may be properly grouped at both extremes of the curve of distribution. They as compared with the girls are brighter and more stupid; the girls evidently maintain the average position, assuming of course the records of promotion and repetition as criteria.

Tables 9 a and 9 b throw some light on the question as to the extent to which each of the sixteen half-year grades acts as a stumbling block for those who survive the entire course and each of the fifteen for those who reach 8 A; and each of the fourteen grades for the 7 B pupils, etc., down through all of the grammar grades including 4 A and 4 B.

The facts will be clearer, however, from the two following tables. Table 10 a is the statement of the aggregate representing the records of 1,312 pupils in the six schools. Table 10 b gives the same facts in per cents.

In cases where a boy or girl was left back once in one grade and once in another, records are made in both places, the same as if the records of two pupils, each showing one non-promotion, were given. If a pupil is left back twice in one grade the record counts as a double score in that grade, in the same way as the records of two individuals who are left back in that grade would count. It is for this reason that Tables 10 a and 10 b do not seem at first glance to tally with Tables 8 a and 8 b. In order to check up Table 10 a turn to Table 8 a and note the following: For example, in 8 B there are 20 left back once which means 20 records; 21 left back twice, or 42 records; 2 left back three times, or 6 records; 3 left back four times, or 12 records, and 1 left back five times to count as 5 records. The sum of 20 + 42 + 6 + 12 + 5, or 85 records, is the same as the sum total of non-promotions in grade 8 B, as recorded in the next to the last column of Table 10 a.

TABLE 10a

Grade Distribution of Non-Promotion in Aggregate

Grades	8B	8A	7B	7A	6B	6A	5B	5A	4B	4A	3B	3A	2B	2A	1B	1A	Grand Total	
																	No. left back	Total promoted and non-prom.
8B	7	5	8	11	9	7	7	5	3	4	4	5	2	4	2	2	85	121
8A		6	9	14	16	4	6	6	6	5	4	4	0	1	0	1	82	99
7B			18	9	7	12	8	6	4	4	3	6	1	4	2	6	90	130
7A				25	14	15	10	19	12	14	8	6	3	4	3	2	135	165
6B					23	22	27	18	15	16	13	14	9	10	6	4	177	218
6A						24	24	27	19	20	25	14	13	13	3	11	193	238
5B							30	29	20	17	23	17	10	8	8	12	174	241
5A								22	21	31	21	32	29	17	10	19	202	244
4B									26	33	46	33	35	28	22	30	253	321
4A										30	24	37	24	18	13	33	179	257

TABLE 10b

Same in Per Cents

Using Total of Promoted and Non-Promoted as the Base

Grades	8B	8A	7B	7A	6B	6A	5B	5A	4B	4A	3B	3A	2B	2A	1B	1A
	per cent	per cent	per cent	per cent	per cent	per cent	per cent	per cent	per cent	per cent	per cent	per cent	per cent	per cent	per cent	per cent
8B	5.8	4.1	6.6	9.1	7.4	5.8	5.8	4.1	2.5	3.3	3.3	4.1	1.7	3.3	1.7	1.7
8A		6.1	9.1	14.1	16.2	4.0	6.1	6.1	6.1	5.1	4.0	4.0	0.0	1.0	0.0	1.0
7B			13.8	6.9	5.4	9.2	6.2	4.6	3.1	3.1	2.3	4.6	0.8	3.1	1.5	4.6
7A				15.2	8.5	9.1	6.1	11.5	7.3	8.5	4.8	3.6	1.8	2.4	1.8	1.2
6B					10.6	10.1	12.4	8.3	6.9	7.3	6.0	6.4	4.1	4.6	2.8	1.8
6A						10.1	10.1	11.3	8.0	8.4	10.5	5.9	5.5	5.5	1.3	4.6
5B							12.4	12.0	8.3	7.1	9.5	7.1	4.1	3.3	3.3	5.0
5A								9.0	8.6	12.7	8.6	13.1	11.9	7.0	4.1	7.8
4B									8.1	10.3	14.3	10.3	10.9	8.7	6.9	9.3
4A										11.7	9.3	14.4	9.3	7.0	5.1	12.8
Aver.[1]	5.8	5.0	10.0	11.5	9.4	8.7	9.2	9.1	7.1	8.6	8.4	8.3	6.1	5.3	3.4	5.9
Aver. of per cents	5.8	5.1	9.8	11.3	9.6	8.1	8.4	8.4	6.5	7.8	7.3	7.4	5.0	4.6	2.9	5.0

[1] In this row the averages are obtained from Table 10a as follows: For example, there are 11 of those now in 8B who were left back in 7A; 14 now in 8A who were left back in 7A; 9 in 7B left back in 7A; and 25 in 7A left back in 7A. The sum of these is 59. Dividing same by the sum of the total promotions and non-promotions in grades 8B, 8A, 7B, and 7A as recorded in the last column of Table 10a, i.e., 121 + 99 + 130 + 165 = 515; and then changing quotient to per cent one gets 11.5 per cent. This statement of averages is a truer one than that made in the bottom row of Table 10b as the latter states merely the averages of gross per cents and in doing so weights all grades alike.

Reading from Table 10 b it is seen, concerning those now in 8 B of the initial starters, that 5.8 per cent represents the amount of non-promotion in grade 8 B; 4.1 per cent in grade 8 A; 6.6 per cent in grade 7 B; 9.1 per cent in grade 7 A; 7.4 per cent in grade 6 B, etc., . . . to 1.7 per cent in grade 1 A. Again concerning those now in 8 A, there was a non-promotion of 6.1 per cent in 8 A; 9.1 per cent in 7 B; 14.1 per cent in 7 A, etc., . . . to 1 per cent in 1 A. In like manner, the other grammar grades may be interpreted.

In fine, it may be said concerning those pupils who are now in grade 8 B that the retention in grade 8 B amounts to about one in seventeen; of those who are in 8 B or are in 8 A, it is about one in twenty in the 8 A grade; of those in or beyond 7 B it is about one in ten in grade 7 B; about one in nine in 7 A, etc.

To account for the low percentages in the first and second grades is difficult. One may contend that the memory of the pupil in the higher grade is at fault, that he is more inclined to forget that he was left back in 1 A or 1 B than in the other grades. While this is possible, it certainly does not seem probable as the entire cause. Perhaps it may be due to the fact that the number of incoming new pupils is, as a rule, quite large, and in consequence there is the necessity for promoting freely in the lowest grades of the school to afford sitting room for the new arrivals. Again it may be that many "under-age" pupils enter the 1 A or 1 B grades and, after a short time, are taken out by their parents on account of the strain and placed in the kindergarten or are kept at home for the rest of the year. These pupils, if asked later in school life to state the grades in which they were left back, would not be inclined to say that they were "held over" in 1 A or 1 B, provided that on their second trial which covered a full term, they passed through these grades successfully. And it does seem reasonable to justify their attitude in this matter.

Turning to Table 10 b again one notes the large per cents in the seventh grades. This seems to indicate that these grades are the chief stumbling blocks, serving to delay the normal progress of a considerable number and so acting with telling effect as the final weeding-out process of the incapable.

Of course it may be argued that whereas about one-half of the pupils in the seventh grades (see Table 2) are fourteen years or more, in consequence the desire to drop out and go to work, coupled with a consequent indifference to the work in these grades, makes for this high rate of "hold-overs," especially when the said pupils are not permitted by their parents to leave school. On the other hand, does not the relative time manifestation of this final selective action seem to be the natural course of events in the high school and the college as well as in the elementary school? Once a student has reached the senior year of his course, one may safely say that he will almost invariably be graduated at the end of the year, the next to the last year functioning as the ultimate selective force.

The following comparative grade study uses data furnished in Table 10 b. Comparing those who are now in the sixth grades with those now in the fourth grades as to the number of times left back, say in the third grades, this table shows:

Grades......	3B per cent	3A per cent
In 6B grade.........	6.0	6.4
In 6A grade.........	10.5	5.9
Median..........	6.2	

Grades......	3B per cent	3A per cent
In 4B grade......	14.3	10.3
In 4A grade......	9.3	14.4
Median......	12.3	

Generally speaking, then, this means that of those who are now in the sixth grades about 1 in 15 was left back in the third grade; whereas of those who are in the fourth grades the ratio of retention increases to approximately 1 in 8. The differences become more marked as we compare grades farther apart. To illustrate, of those now in the eighth grades it will be found that only 1 in 25 was left back in the third grades.

Now comparing the eighth and seventh grades with the fifth and fourth grades with respect to non-promotion in the third grades, one notes the following distribution:

Grades......	3B per cent	3A per cent
8B grade..........	3.3	4.1
8A grade..........	4.0	4.0
7B grade..........	2.3	4.6
7A grade..........	4.8	3.6
Median..........	4.0	

Grades......	3B per cent	3A per cent
5B grade..........	9.5	7.1
5A grade..........	8.6	13.1
4B grade..........	14.3	10.3
4A grade..........	9.3	14.4
Median.........	9.9	

That is, the ratio of non-promotion in the third grades of those initial starters who are now in the seventh and eighth grades to those now in the fourth and fifth grades, is as 4 is to 10 approximately.

Assuming the proper correction to be made for errors of memory in those cases where the card records were not obtainable and the teachers and classmates were unable to check up the doubtful pupils' statements, it seems justifiable to conclude that intrinsically the grades one to seven in this district are progressively harder. For the same pupil, retardation becomes more probable grade by grade till the eighth. The common view that retardation is chiefly a matter of the primary grades is certainly false for these schools, the fact being that the many pupils who are retarded in grades one to four would be retarded still oftener if they continued in school.

CHAPTER III

ELIZABETH, N. J. 1,088 CASES

In Elizabeth, N. J., five schools were visited during the month of March, 1910. These schools typify conditions in all sections of the city. They represent the entire number of schools having the complete series of grades from the first to the eighth inclusive. The records of 1,088 pupils were obtained and tabulated according to the method employed in Chapter II. The numbers of pupils on register in the schools studied are approximately: School G, 600; School H, 1,600; School I, 900; School J, 500; School K, 700.

The Migration of Pupils

Table 11 shows the per cents of initial starters.[1] Subtracting these per cents from 100 per cent one may determine the relative amount of migration in these schools plus, as was previously explained, the percentage of those pupils who were admitted as absolutely new pupils in or beyond the second grade.

TABLE 11

Per Cents of Initial Starters

Schools	G	H	I	J	K	Aver.
Grades	per cent	per cent	per cent	per cent	per cent	per cent
Eighth	8	61	7	19	55	32.9
Seventh	9	58	32	26	44	33.6
Sixth	16	57	33	46	35	37.0
Fifth	37	60	54	53	38	51.5
Fourth	43	48	51	35	41	44.8
Average	23	57	35	36	43	40.8

[1] Method of obtaining these per cents is explained on page 21, chap. II.

From Table 11 it is seen that on the average 40.8 per cent[1] of the pupils in grades four through eight of the schools of Elizabeth began their work in the first grade of the schools they now attend. The range is from 23 per cent in School G to 57 per cent in School H. Grades 6, 7, and 8 average below 40.8 per cent, grades 4 and 5 are above, indicating the lack of persistency on the part of the initial starters as they advance to the higher grammar grades.

The Age-Grade Relations of the 1,088 Initial Starters

The distribution of pupils according to age at the time of entrance to the present grade is shown in the following table. The percentages of retardation are printed in the last column.

TABLE 12

Five Schools. Age Distribution. Aggregate 1,088 Cases

Grades	8	9	10	11	12	13	14	15	16	Total	Above Normal Age	
											No.	Per cent
Eighth					10	40	42	31	7	130	80	61.5
Seventh				10	37	58	46	18	3	172	125	72.7
Sixth			14	34	81	48	33	6	2	218	170	78.0
Fifth		8	46	107	99	62	27			349	295	84.5
Fourth	4	37	65	48	41	13	11			219	178	81.3
							Total.......			1,088	Cases	

In the eighth grade 61.5 per cent of the pupils are reported as being "over-age," assuming 13 years to 13 years 11 months as the normal entrance age to the eighth grade; 72.7 per cent in grade 7; 78.0 per cent in grade 6; 84.5 per cent in grade 5; and 81.3 per cent in grade 4. These percentages are extremely high and show a marked progressive decrease from the fifth grade to the eighth grade inclusive. Counting only those pupils in the fourth grade as "over-age" who exceed the age limit of 9

[1] This percentage is derived by dividing the entire number of records obtained by the total register of the five schools (grades 4 to 8 only) at the time of visitation.

years 0 months to 9 years 11 months inclusive by one or more years and measuring the other grades accordingly these percentages of retardation would lower to: Eighth grade, 29.2 per cent; seventh grade, 39.0 per cent; sixth grade, 40.8 per cent; fifth grade, 53.9 per cent; and fourth grade, 51.6 per cent.

The distribution of the retarded pupils in these grades according to sex is shown in the table and charts following.

TABLE 13

FIVE SCHOOLS. AGE-GRADE TABLE SHOWING SEX DISTRIBUTION

Boys in plain type. Girls in italics.

Grades	8	9	10	11	12	13	14	15	16	Total	Above Normal Age No.	Above Normal Age Per cent
Eighth					*6* 4	*21* 19	*25* 17	*10* 21	*2* 5	*64* 66	*37* 43	*57.8* 65.2
Seventh				*6* 4	*22* 15	*27* 31	*21* 25	*5* 13	*3* 0	*84* 88	*56* 69	*66.7* 78.4
Sixth			*8* 6	*19* 15	*47* 34	*27* 21	*12* 21	*2* 4	*0* 2	*115* 103	*88* 82	*76.5* 79.6
Fifth		*6* 2	*31* 15	*55* 52	*52* 47	*29* 33	*11* 16			*184* 165	*147* 148	*79.9* 89.7
Fourth	*3* 1	*22* 15	*33* 32	*28* 20	*17* 24	*5* 8	*4* 7			*112* 107	*87* 91	*77.7* 85.0
Total..........										*559* 529	Girls Boys	

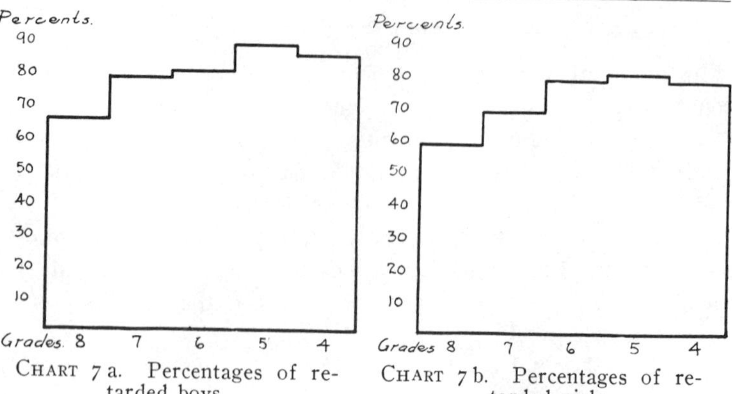

CHART 7 a. Percentages of retarded boys

CHART 7 b. Percentages of retarded girls

In the schools of Elizabeth there seems to be no doubt concerning sex difference in retardation. In every instance as shown in the preceding table the boys are more retarded than the girls. The median for the 529 cases (boys) in grades 4 through 8 is 79.6; whereas for the 559 cases (girls) it is 76.5. In the two upper grammar grades the boys as compared with the girls show relatively more "over-ageness" than in the two lower grades. With both sexes the same progressive increase in retardation is noticeable (see charts 5 a and 5 b) in descending from the eighth to the fourth grade. Were the theoretical age limit for the fourth grade taken to extend from 9 to 11 years, for the fifth grade from 10 to 12 years, for the sixth grade from 11 to 13 years, etc., the "over-age" boys in each case would again be recorded in larger numbers.

Table 14 shows the distribution of the 1,088 cases according to age at the time of their entrance to the first grade of the school in which they now attend.

TABLE 14

AGE DISTRIBUTION OF 1,088 PUPILS AT TIME OF ENTRANCE TO THE FIRST GRADE

Schools	5	6	7	8 or more	Total	Above Normal Age	
						No.	Per cent
G	5	36	60	32	133	92	69.2
H	17	145	246	120	528	366	69.3
I	4	62	65	33	164	98	59.8
J	3	32	51	24	110	75	68.2
K	5	37	74	37	153	111	72.5
Total	34	312	496	246	1,088	742	68.2

Approximately 68 per cent of the cases studied were "overage" at the time of entrance to the first grade. Relative to this exceptionally high figure, the superintendent explained that the parents were encouraged during the past five years by the medical officials of the city in public circulars and otherwise, not to send their children to school before the age of seven. This accounts for the fact that of the five cities reported on in this study, Elizabeth records by far the largest percentage of initial "over-ageness."[1] The modal entrance age as shown in the foregoing distribution is clearly in the group, 7 years to 7 years 11 months inclusive.

The distribution of these 1,088 pupils at the time of their school entrance is again recorded in Table 15. This table is more valuable in that it shows also the distribution by grades.

From the percentages of "over-ageness" at the time of entrance to the first grade, as read in the last column of Table 15, one notes that in grades 4 and 5 such "over-ageness" is at a maximum. Evidently the fact aforementioned concerning the attitude of the medical men largely accounts for these high percentages. The upper grades show less pupils above normal age. Whereas it is certainly wrong in comparing Tables 15 and 12 to say positively that 61.5 per cent now in the eighth grade are "over-age," 56.2 per cent of the eighth grade pupils were "over-age" at the time of entrance to the first grade, therefore approximately 85 per cent of those who are "over-age" now are so because of "over-ageness" at the time of school entrance, still it may be true and is highly probable that the vast majority of the retarded pupils in the Elizabeth schools are so in consequence of their initial "over-ageness" on starting school.

Comparison of sexes in the matter of age-record at the time of their entrance to the first grades is shown in Table 16 and accompanying charts.

Of the 529 boys whose records were taken, 72.2 per cent were found to be over 6 years 11 months when they entered the first grade; of the 559 girl initial starters, 61.5 per cent were thus "over-age." Just as was pointed out in comparing the boys and girls classified as retarded in their present grades (see page 43), the boys in each grade show here larger percentages above the assumed normal entrance age.

In the eighth grade whereas 65.2 per cent (Table 13) of the boys are above normal age, a still larger proportion (74.2 per cent) of these boys were "over-age" when they began school. In all the other grades the percentages of initial "over-ageness" closely approximate the present "over-ageness" in the case of

[1] See Chapter VII, Table 51.

TABLE 15

AGE-GRADE DISTRIBUTION OF 1,088 PUPILS AT TIME OF ENTRANCE TO THE FIRST GRADE

Ages	Five Years					Six Years					Seven Years					Eight Years or More					Total Cases	Above Normal Age	
Schools	G	H	I	J	K	G	H	I	J	K	G	H	I	J	K	G	H	I	J	K		No.	Per cent
Grades Eighth	1	2	2	1	0	4	28	8	4	7	6	34	4	1	3	3	17	2	0	3	130	73	56.2
Seventh	0	7	1	1	2	6	20	19	8	12	8	50	6	3	3	5	11	4	2	4	172	96	55.8
Sixth	1	3	0	1	0	9	38	8	5	4	13	51	16	12	10	7	20	7	5	8	218	149	68.3
Fifth	2	3	1	0	1	11	37	17	8	9	17	69	20	26	46	1c	35	11	10	16	349	260	74.5
Fourth	1	2	0	0	2	6	22	10	7	5	16	42	19	9	12	7	37	9	7	6	219	164	74.9
Total	5	17	4	3	5	36	145	62	32	37	60	246	65	51	74	32	120	33	24	37	1,088	742	68.2

TABLE 16

Age-Grade Sex Distribution of 1,088 Pupils at Time of Entrance to First Grade

Boys in plain type. Girls in italics.

Ages	Five Years					Six Years					Seven Years					Eight Years or More					Total Cases	Above Normal Age	
Schools	G	H	I	J	K	G	H	I	J	K	G	H	I	J	K	G	H	I	J	K		No.	Per cent
Grades																							
Eighth	*1*	*1*	*1*	*0*	*0*	*3*	*20*	*6*	*3*	*5*	*1*	*13*	*1*	*0*	*1*	*1*	*5*	*1*	*0*	*1*	*64*	*24*	*37.5*
	0	1	1	1	0	1	8	2	1	2	5	21	3	1	2	2	12	1	0	2	66	49	74.2
Seventh	*0*	*4*	*1*	*0*	*1*	*4*	*10*	*9*	*4*	*7*	*3*	*22*	*2*	*1*	*1*	*3*	*6*	*2*	*1*	*3*	*84*	*44*	*52.4*
	0	3	0	1	1	2	10	10	4	5	5	28	4	2	2	2	5	2	1	1	88	52	59.1
Sixth	*1*	*2*	*0*	*1*	*0*	*5*	*21*	*5*	*4*	*2*	*7*	*23*	*8*	*6*	*5*	*3*	*11*	*5*	*2*	*4*	*115*	*74*	*64.3*
	0	1	0	0	0	4	17	3	1	2	6	28	8	6	5	4	9	2	3	4	103	75	72.8
Fifth	*2*	*2*	*1*	*0*	*1*	*8*	*22*	*12*	*6*	*6*	*7*	*31*	*8*	*13*	*24*	*5*	*16*	*7*	*4*	*9*	*184*	*124*	*67.4*
	0	1	0	0	0	3	15	5	2	3	10	38	12	13	22	5	19	4	6	7	165	136	82.5
Fourth	*1*	*1*	*0*	*0*	*1*	*4*	*13*	*6*	*4*	*4*	*6*	*20*	*9*	*3*	*6*	*4*	*19*	*4*	*4*	*3*	*112*	*78*	*69.6*
	0	1	0	0	1	2	9	4	3	1	10	22	10	6	6	3	18	5	3	3	107	86	80.4
Total	*5*	*10*	*3*	*1*	*3*	*24*	*86*	*38*	*21*	*24*	*24*	*109*	*28*	*23*	*37*	*16*	*57*	*19*	*11*	*20*	*559*	*344*	*61.5*
	0	7	1	2	2	12	59	24	11	13	36	137	37	28	37	16	63	14	13	17	529	398	75.2

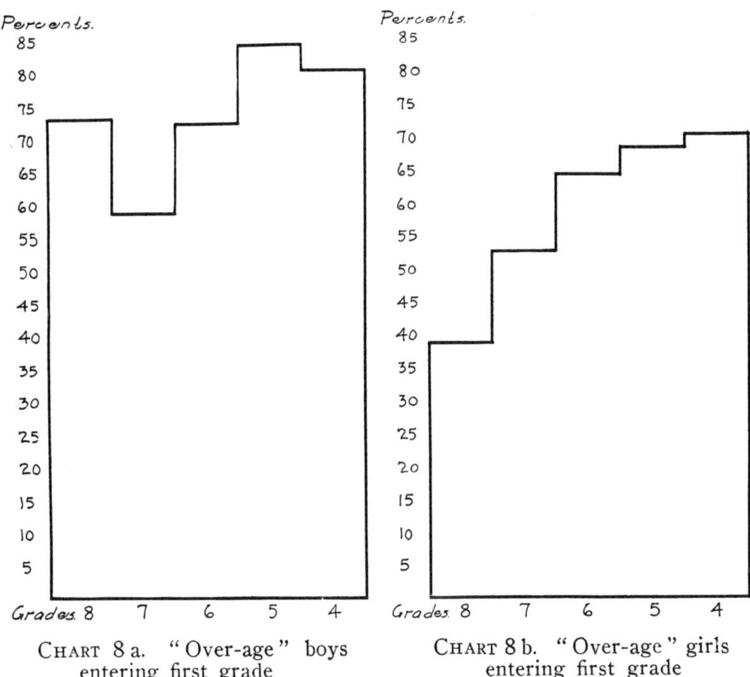

CHART 8 a. "Over-age" boys entering first grade

CHART 8 b. "Over-age" girls entering first grade

the boys. Some such statement then as the following is justifiable: Whereas the boys are more retarded than the girls in the schools of Elizabeth, such retardation is probably due more to initial retardation rather than to failure to pass regularly through the grades. As for the boys this would seem at first glance to argue the advisability of encouraging them to enter school later in years. Table 18 b (page 49) however disproves this.

That the boys are more variable than the girls in this instance is again evident from the appended diagrams. Note the progressive increase in initial "over-ageness" of the girls in grades 8 through 4 (Chart 8 b). The same steady increase in present "over-ageness" is to be noted in Chart 7 b, page 42.

THE INCIDENCE OF RETARDATION

The numbers of repeating and non-repeating pupils of the 1,088 children investigated are shown in Table 17 a. These figures are changed to per cents in Table 17 b.

TABLE 17a

Five Schools. Aggregate 1,088 Cases

Left Back	Fourth	Fifth	Sixth	Seventh	Eighth
None	133	176	133	113	92
One	56	127	62	40	29
Two	22	38	20	17	7
Three	6	6	3	2	1
Four	2	2	0	0	1
Total Left Back	86	173	85	59	38
Total Cases	219	349	218	172	130

TABLE 17b

Same Converted to Per Cent Equivalents

Left Back	Fourth	Fifth	Sixth	Seventh	Eighth
	per cent	per cent	per cent	per cent	per cent
None	61	50	61	66	71
One	26	36	28	23	22
Two	10	11	9	10	5
Three	3	2	1	1	1
Four	1	1	0	0	1
Total Left Back	39	50	39	34	29

In the five grades tabulated, the mode in each case is in the "no-time" group. Although the percentages of retardation are highest in the Elizabeth schools, the percentages of pupils repeating during their entire school life are lowest when compared with those of the other four cities. This again seems to point to the fact that the present considerable "over-ageness" in the schools of this city is due largely to "over-ageness" at the time of entrance to the first grade.

The sex distribution of repeaters and non-repeaters is shown next in tables and diagrams.

TABLE 18a

PUPILS REPEATING AND NON-REPEATING DURING SCHOOL LIFE

Boys in plain type. Girls in italics.

Left Back	Fourth	Fifth	Sixth	Seventh	Eighth
None	*71* 62	*102* 74	*83* 50	*56* 57	*47* 45
One	*32* 24	*60* 67	*27* 35	*18* 22	*14* 15
Two	*6* 16	*18* 20	*5* 15	*9* 8	*2* 5
Three	*3* 3	*2* 4	*0* 3	*1* 1	*0* 1
Four	*0* 2	*2* 0	*0* 0	*0* 0	*1* 0
Total Left Back	*41* 45	*82* 91	*32* 53	*28* 31	*17* 21
Total Cases	*112* 107	*184* 165	*115* 103	*84* 88	*64* 66

TABLE 18b

SAME CONVERTED TO PER CENT EQUIVALENTS

Boys in plain type. Girls in italics.

Left Back	Fourth	Fifth	Sixth	Seventh	Eighth
	per cent	per cent	per cent	per cent	per cent
None	*63.4* 57.9	*55.4* 44.8	*72.2* 48.5	*66.7* 64.8	*73.4* 68.2
One	*28.6* 22.4	*32.6* 40.6	*23.5* 34.0	*21.4* 25.0	*21.9* 22.7
Two	*5.4* 15.0	*9.8* 12.1	*4.3* 14.6	*10.7* 9.1	*3.1* 7.6
Three	*2.7* 2.8	*1.1* 2.5	*0.0* 2.9	*1.2* 1.2	*0.0* 1.5
Four	*0.0* 1.9	*1.1* 0.0	*0.0* 0.0	*0.0* 0.0	*1.6* 0.0
Total Left Back	*36.6* 42.1	*44.6* 56.4	*27.8* 51.5	*33.3* 35.2	*26.6* 31.8

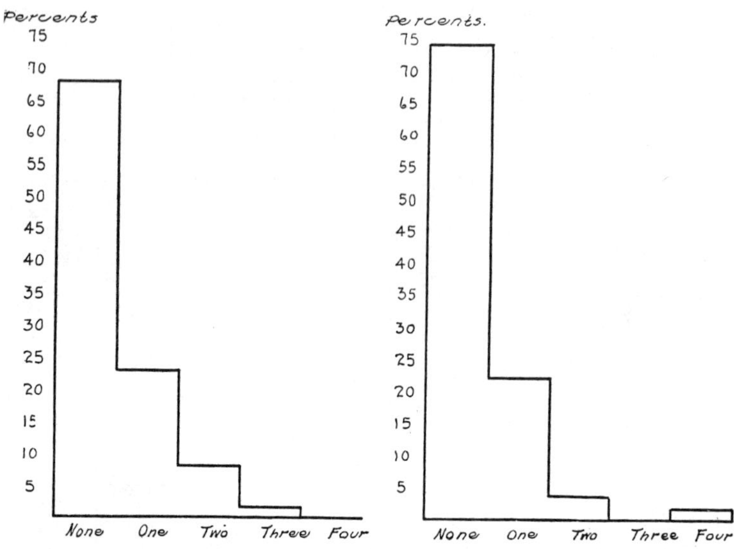

CHART 9 a. Eighth grade boys. Repeaters and non-repeaters during school life

CHART 9 b. Eighth grade girls. Repeaters and non-repeaters during school life

The girls recorded in these five schools are unquestionably brighter than the boys if one measures mental ability on the basis of the relative frequency of promotions and non-promotions. In the fourth through the eighth grades the ratio of the regularly promoted girls to the total number of girls promoted and non-promoted exceeds that of the boys similarly figured. The boys in almost every grade are also left back more frequently once, twice, and three times. The two girls in the fifth grade and the one in the eighth grade (see Table 18 a) repeating four times are quite exceptional.

In the eighth grade, it is seen from Table 18 b that 73.4 per cent of all the girls studied, were never left back during their entire school life; 21.9 per cent were left back once; and 3.1 per cent, twice. Of the boys 68.2 per cent were promoted regularly since school entrance; 22.7 per cent failed once; and 7.6 per cent failed twice. Again it would seem that the selected girls who reach the graduating class must be credited with better records although the differences are not so marked as in the lower grades, especially the sixth. Judged accordingly, the girls here by far outstrip the boys in mental ability. The charts show respectively the percentages of promoted and non-promoted eighth grade boys and girls. The one glaring fact is the large percentages of regularly advancing pupils in both cases.

Relative to the grade distribution of the repeating pupils, Table 19 a in actual numbers and Table 19 b in per cents show plainly such incidence of retardation.

TABLE 19a

GRADE DISTRIBUTION OF NON-PROMOTION IN AGGREGATE

Grades	Eighth	Seventh	Sixth	Fifth	Fourth	Third	Second	First	Grand Total	
									No. Left back	Total Prom. and Non-Prom.
Eighth	8	13	3	3	6	7	5	5	50	142
Seventh		24	9	8	5	8	11	15	80	193
Sixth			30	25	24	13	9	10	111	244
Fifth				77	49	41	33	29	229	405
Fourth					46	37	24	19	126	259

TABLE 19b

SAME IN PER CENTS

Using Total of Promoted and Non-Promoted as the Base

Grades	Eighth	Seventh	Sixth	Fifth	Fourth	Third	Second	First
	per cent	per cent	per cent	per cent	per cent	per cent	per cent	per cent
Eighth	5.6	9.2	2.1	2.1	4.2	4.9	3.5	3.5
Seventh		12.4	4.7	4.1	2.6	4.1	5.7	7.8
Sixth			12.3	10.2	9.8	5.3	3.7	4.1
Fifth				19.0	12.1	10.1	8.1	7.2
Fourth					17.8	10.4	9.3	7.3
Aver.	5.6	11.0	7.3	11.5	10.5	8.5	6.6	6.3

The progressive increase of retardation till the sixth grade is manifest in the bottom row of average percentages, Table 19 b, computed in the manner explained in the preceding chapter on page 36. The distribution curve in the case of the school children of Elizabeth would show two distinct high levels, one in the fifth grade and the other in the seventh. It is reasonable to suppose then that a large number of pupils are eliminated in the difficult fourth and fifth grades and that those pupils who remain find little trouble in accomplishing the sixth grade work but are subjected to the final selective test when they enter the seventh grade. The successful seventh grade scholars then pass into the easy eighth grade, from which nearly all at the close of the year are permitted to graduate.

Comparing percentages of eighth, sixth, and fourth grade pupils with respect to their records of failure in the third grade, Table 19 b shows:

	Third Grade per cent
In eighth grade	4.9
In sixth grade	5.3
In fourth grade	10.4

Approximately twice as many pupils in the fourth grade as compared with either the sixth or eighth grade are left back in the third grade. In grades eight and six about 1 in 20 were "held over" in the third grade, whereas of the fourth grade pupils as many as 1 in 10 failed in the lower grade.

The relative amounts of retention in the third grade of the eighth and seventh grade pupils and those of the fifth and fourth grades are:

	Third Grade per cent		Third Grade per cent
In eighth grade	4.9	In fifth grade	10.1
In seventh grade	4.1	In fourth grade	10.4
Median	4.5	*Median*	10.3

In fine, then, it may be said that the fourth or fifth grade pupil is left back in the third grade more than twice as often as the eighth or seventh grade pupil. The fact that the fourth, fifth, and seventh grades in this city school system are the most difficult for the children who have gone through them, is undeniable. The high percentage of repetition in the seventh grade indicates this grade to be the ultimate selective force. Those who just survive the fourth and fifth grades, were they to remain, would most probably be "held over" again in the seventh grade if not eliminated altogether.

CHAPTER IV

PATERSON, N. J. 1,246 CASES

The five schools of Paterson, N. J., reported in this chapter furnished records of 1,246 initial starters. Only the grammar grade pupils are considered and these are tabulated as in New York City in half-yearly grades. The "A" classes, however, are the upper and the "B" classes the lower grades in the Paterson school system. School O with 1,500 pupils registered represents the largest school and School N with a registry of 900 pupils, the smallest at the time of visitation during the months of March and April, 1910.

The Migration of Pupils

The approximate percentages of initial starters now in the grammar grades are shown in Table 20.

TABLE 20

Per Cents of Initial Starters

Schools	L	M	N	O	P	Average
Grades	per cent	per cent	per cent	per cent	per cent	per cent
8A	62	39	37	52	49	48.3
8B	44	57	44	60	44	51.0
7A	33	58	38	49	43	47.4
7B	67	60	41	60	45	55.4
6A	46	47	49	52	53	50.3
6B	38	47	39	41	28	40.1
5A	46	55	45	59	36	49.1
5B	55	43	61	53	37	50.3
Average	48	51	45	54	43	48.9

Accordingly 48.9 per cent of the grammar grade pupils registered in the five schools are rated as initial starters. That is, approximately half the number of grammar grade children in the Paterson schools must have either migrated to the schools they now attend from other schools in Paterson or from other cities or else must have been admitted as new pupils in their present school in a higher grade than the first. This would seem to be the tendency in all the grammar grades with but slight deviation. The largest school, School O, with .52 in 8 A and .60 in 8 B and an average for all the grammar grades of .54 excels all the others in percentages of initial starters.

The Age-Grade Relations of the 1,246 Initial Starters

The 1,246 pupils tabulated in the following distribution are segregated with respect to age at the time of entrance to the present grade.

TABLE 21

Five Schools. Age Distribution. Aggregate 1,246 Cases

Grades	8	9	10	11	12	13	14	15	16	Total	Above Normal Age	
											No.	Per cent
8A					17	50	37	17	8	129	62	48.1
8B				3	42	53	39	9	1	147	49	33.3
7A			1	15	63	53	28	2		162	83	51.2
7B			10	44	58	52	20	2		186	74	39.8
6A		3	14	57	59	29	14			176	102	58.0
6B		3	19	56	35	21	6			140	62	44.3
5A		13	38	46	23	16	3			139	88	63.3
5B	7	41	59	27	13	18	2			167	60	35.9
							Total........			1,246	Cases	

The percentages of "over-ageness" in the grades of the Paterson schools are seen to be relatively small but considerable variation is manifest. The fifth and sixth grades show higher percentages than the seventh and eighth. The upper seventh grade recording 51.2 per cent as above normal age is significant. Those that do reach this grade are probably "held back" here more than in the preceding grades. (See Table 21.)

Assuming 14 years to 14 years 11 months inclusive instead of 13 years to 13 years 11 months inclusive as the normal entrance age to the eighth grade, the percentages of "over-age" pupils would decrease to: 8 A grade, 19.4 per cent; 8 B grade, 6.8 per cent; 7 A grade, 18.5 per cent; 7 B grade, 11.8 per cent; 6 A grade, 24.4 per cent; 6 B grade, 14.3 per cent; 5 A grade, 30.2 per cent; 5 B grade, 19.8 per cent.

Note that in each instance the lower "B" grades show smaller percentages of retarded pupils than the upper "A" grades for

TABLE 22

FIVE SCHOOLS. AGE-GRADE TABLE SHOWING SEX DISTRIBUTION

Boys in plain type. Girls in italics.

Grades	8	9	10	11	12	13	14	15	16	Total	Above Normal Age	
											No.	Per cent
8A					*12* 5	*32* 18	*15* 22	*8* 9	*3* 5	*70* 59	*26* 26	*37.1* 44.1
8B				*1* 2	*22* 20	*26* 27	*15* 24	*1* 8	*0* 1	*65* 82	*16* 33	*24.6* 40.2
7A			*1* 0	*9* 6	*38* 25	*32* 21	*16* 12	*1* 1		*97* 65	*49* 34	*50.5* 52.3
7B			*5* 5	*23* 21	*25* 33	*25* 27	*8* 12	*1* 1		*87* 99	*34* 40	*39.1* 40.4
6A		*2* 1	*8* 6	*29* 28	*23* 36	*18* 11	*9* 5			*89* 87	*50* 52	*56.2* 59.8
6B		*2* 1	*10* 9	*33* 23	*12* 23	*10* 11	*0* 6			*67* 73	*22* 40	*32.8* 54.8
5A		*9* 4	*18* 20	*29* 17	*10* 13	*9* 7	*2* 1			*77* 62	*50* 38	*64.9* 61.3
5B	*4* 3	*26* 15	*24* 35	*11* 16	*5* 8	*7* 11	*0* 2			*77* 90	*23* 37	*29.9* 41.1
							Total......			*629* 617	Girls Boys	

the reason that the same theoretical normal age was assumed for the lower half-yearly grade as for the higher. The same holds true of the New York City schools with the single exception of the eighth grades. (See Chapter II, page 22.) If, for example, the age limit for the 8 B grade were taken to extend from 13 years to 13 years 11 months inclusive, it would perhaps have been fairer to have taken 13 years 6 months to 14 years 5 months inclusive as the normal entrance age to the 8 A grade.

Table 22 and the graphic illustrations represent the sex distribution of the "under-age," "normal," and "over-age" pupils, the diagrams referring only to the last group. (Chart 10 a and 10 b which refer to Table 22 are found on page 60.)

From the preceding age-grade table one learns that with the exception of grade 5 A, the boys are retarded much more often than the girls. The median in the case of the former for the eight grades tabulated would be 48.2; in the case of the latter, only 38.1. The difference is most marked in the two eighth grades. The boys as compared with the girls who do reach these grades are much older. The larger ratios of "over-age" boys would still hold in all grades excepting 7 A and 6 A were the age limit raised a year in each case. The charts illustrate plainly that in the matter of retardation the grammar grade girls of the Paterson schools are much more variable than the boys.

The following table records the age distribution of these grammar grade pupils at the time of their entrance to the 1 B grade of the school in which they now are.

Of the 1,246 initial starters, 286 or only 23 per cent were over 6 years 11 months when they entered the 1 B grade of the school. Just as Paterson with no exception has less retardation in its grammar grades than the other cities, it likewise shows considerably less initial "over-ageness" of its local beginners. Whereas the largest school, School O, had the largest percentage of initial starters (see page 53), Table 23 records this school as having the largest percentage of "over-ageness" on the part of such pupils. School N with next to the smallest percentage in Table 20 holds in Table 23 the minimum record. The median entrance age in the Paterson schools would fall in the group 6 years to 6 years 11 months inclusive, the normal entrance age considered throughout in this special study.

TABLE 23

AGE DISTRIBUTION OF 1,246 PUPILS AT TIME OF ENTRANCE TO 1B GRADE

Schools	5	6	7	8	9	10	Total	Above Normal Age	
								No.	Per cent
L	84	69	39	8	5	0	205	52	25.4
M	122	84	43	4	3	0	256	50	19.8
N	76	66	26	7	0	0	175	33	18.9
O	158	137	67	22	15	4	403	108	26.8
P	74	90	39	3	1	0	207	43	20.8
Total	514	446	214	44	24	4	1,246	286	23.0

Table 24 shows the same pupils considered in Table 23 distributed according to present grade and entrance age to the 1 B grade.

Comparing this table with Table 21 one can find little reason to explain the present grade "over-ageness" on the basis of the initial "over-ageness" of the beginners. In grade 7 A, Table 21 records nearly the highest percentage of retardation; whereas Table 24 shows almost the smallest percentage: 19.8 per cent of the present 7 A pupils as "over-age" when they entered school. On the other hand Table 24 tells us that the highest proportion, 30.6 per cent of the present 7 B pupils, were above normal age at the time of their entrance to grade 1 B; Table 21 records only 39.8 per cent or the sixth from the highest percentage of present "over-age" pupils.

The sex distribution of these initial starters is stated in Table 25 and the graphic illustrations of the "over-age" boys and girls entering grade 1 B are shown on page 60 (Charts 11 a and 11 b).

In total, 23.5 per cent of the girls as opposed to 22.4 per cent of the boys were above 6 years 11 months when they entered school. Just as the girls showed the largest percentages of re-

TABLE 24

AGE-GRADE DISTRIBUTION OF 1,246 PUPILS AT TIME OF ENTRANCE TO 1B GRADE

Ages	Five Years					Six Years					Seven Years					Eight Years					Nine Years or More					Total Cases	Above Normal Age	
School Grades	L	M	N	O	P	L	M	N	O	P	L	M	N	O	P	L	M	N	O	P	L	M	N	O	P		No.	Per cent
8A	9	11	2	15	10	12	4	9	20	6	3	1	5	9	5	0	1	0	5	1	0	0	0	0	1	129	31	24.0
8B	6	11	4	24	13	3	13	10	19	17	7	4	2	3	7	0	0	0	1	0	0	0	0	3	0	147	27	18.4
7A	6	24	5	23	6	6	22	8	19	11	1	10	2	10	2	0	0	1	3	1	0	0	0	2	0	162	32	19.8
7B	15	16	0	27	13	8	7	7	21	15	9	7	9	14	7	0	0	0	4	0	0	0	0	7	0	186	57	30.6
6A	9	10	8	26	19	11	6	9	21	15	3	5	4	9	12	2	1	1	3	0	0	0	0	2	0	176	42	23.9
6B	10	22	17	10	3	14	13	9	10	6	3	7	2	6	2	2	0	2	0	0	1	0	0	1	0	140	26	18.6
5A	20	9	8	12	4	9	11	5	14	9	6	4	2	10	3	1	1	0	2	1	3	1	0	4	0	139	38	27.3
5B	9	19	32	21	6	6	8	9	13	11	7	5	0	6	1	3	1	3	4	0	1	2	0	0	0	167	33	19.8
Total	84	122	76	158	74	69	84	66	137	90	39	43	26	67	39	8	4	7	22	3	5	3	0	19	1	1,246	286	23.0

TABLE [illegible]

AGE-GRADE SEX DISTRIBUTION OF 1,246 PUPILS AT TIME OF ENTRANCE TO 1B GRADE

Boys in plain type. Girls in italics.

Ages	Five Years					Six Years					Seven Years					Eight Years					Nine Years or More					Total Cases	Above Normal Age	
School	L	M	N	O	P	L	M	N	O	P	L	M	N	O	P	L	M	N	O	P	L	M	N	O	P		No.	Per cent
Grades 8A	*8*	*5*	*1*	*13*	*1*	*7*	*1*	*7*	*11*	*1*	*2*	*0*	*4*	*6*	*0*	*0*	*1*	*0*	*2*	*0*	*0*	*0*	*0*	*0*	*0*	*70*	*15*	*21.4*
	1	6	1	2	9	5	3	2	9	5	1	1	1	3	5	0	0	0	3	1	0	0	0	0	1	59	16	27.1
8B	*5*	*6*	*0*	*12*	*7*	*2*	*5*	*5*	*5*	*6*	*1*	*2*	*1*	*2*	*6*	*0*	*0*	*0*	*0*	*0*	*0*	*0*	*0*	*0*	*0*	*65*	*12*	*18.5*
	1	5	4	12	6	1	8	5	14	11	6	2	1	1	1	0	0	0	1	0	0	0	0	3	0	82	15	18.3
7A	*2*	*11*	*2*	*17*	*4*	*4*	*15*	*7*	*11*	*3*	*1*	*9*	*1*	*5*	*1*	*0*	*0*	*1*	*2*	*1*	*0*	*0*	*0*	*0*	*0*	*97*	*21*	*21.6*
	4	13	3	6	2	2	7	1	8	8	0	1	1	5	1	0	0	0	1	0	0	0	0	2	0	65	11	16.9
7B	*8*	*9*	*0*	*14*	*7*	*1*	*4*	*4*	*9*	*6*	*4*	*3*	*2*	*7*	*4*	*0*	*0*	*0*	*2*	*0*	*0*	*0*	*0*	*3*	*0*	*87*	*25*	*28.7*
	7	7	0	13	6	7	3	3	12	9	5	4	7	7	3	0	0	0	2	0	0	0	0	4	0	99	32	32.3
6A	*5*	*1*	*3*	*14*	*9*	*2*	*4*	*4*	*14*	*7*	*1*	*3*	*3*	*7*	*5*	*2*	*0*	*1*	*2*	*0*	*0*	*0*	*0*	*2*	*0*	*89*	*26*	*29.2*
	4	9	5	12	10	9	2	5	7	8	2	2	1	2	7	0	1	0	1	0	0	0	0	0	0	87	16	18.4
6B	*4*	*11*	*4*	*6*	*2*	*6*	*6*	*4*	*5*	*5*	*1*	*3*	*1*	*5*	*2*	*1*	*0*	*0*	*0*	*0*	*1*	*0*	*0*	*0*	*0*	*67*	*14*	*20.9*
	6	11	13	4	1	8	7	5	5	1	2	4	1	1	0	1	0	2	0	0	0	0	0	1	0	73	12	16.4
5A	*12*	*5*	*2*	*6*	*1*	*8*	*5*	*4*	*9*	*5*	*5*	*1*	*1*	*7*	*0*	*1*	*0*	*0*	*2*	*0*	*2*	*0*	*0*	*1*	*0*	*77*	*20*	*26.0*
	8	4	6	6	3	1	6	1	5	4	1	3	1	3	3	0	1	0	0	1	1	1	0	3	0	62	18	29.0
5B	*4*	*9*	*17*	*13*	*1*	*4*	*4*	*2*	*5*	*3*	*5*	*4*	*0*	*0*	*1*	*2*	*0*	*0*	*1*	*0*	*1*	*1*	*0*	*0*	*0*	*77*	*15*	*19.5*
	5	10	15	8	5	2	4	7	8	8	2	1	0	6	0	1	1	3	3	0	0	1	0	0	0	90	18	20.0
Total	*48*	*57*	*29*	*95*	*32*	*34*	*44*	*37*	*69*	*36*	*20*	*25*	*13*	*39*	*19*	*6*	*1*	*2*	*11*	*1*	*4*	*1*	*0*	*6*	*0*	*629*	*148*	*23.5*
	36	65	47	63	42	35	40	29	68	54	19	18	13	28	20	2	3	5	11	2	1	2	0	13	1	617	138	22.4

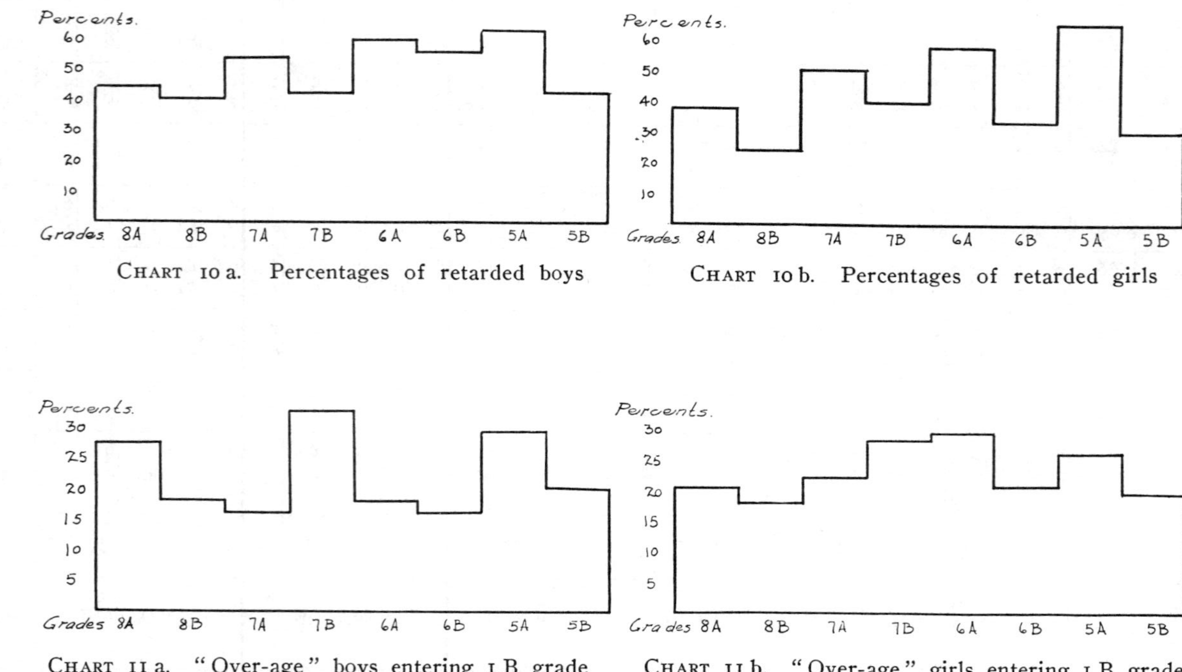

CHART 10 a. Percentages of retarded boys

CHART 10 b. Percentages of retarded girls

CHART 11 a. "Over-age" boys entering 1 B grade

CHART 11 b. "Over-age" girls entering 1 B grade

tardation in the sixth and seventh grades (Table 22), in Table 25 they also show more initial "over-ageness" in these grades.

Whereas the boys are retarded more in the fifth and sixth grades and least in the 7 B grade according to Table 22; in the eighth and the fifth grades and mostly in the 7 B grade, one notes the largest percentages above normal age at the time of school entrance (Table 25). Evidently late entrance with the boys is not so potent a cause of retardation as in the case of the girls. Charts 11 a and 11 b again call attention to the tendency toward greater variability on the part of the boys.

The Incidence of Retardation

Table 26 a represents in numbers the distribution of the 1,246 Paterson school children according as they were or were not left back during their entire school life. Table 26 b reports the same, only the numbers are changed to per cent equivalents.

TABLE 26a

Five Schools. Aggregate 1,246 Cases

Left Back	5B	5A	6B	6A	7B	7A	8B	8A
None	94	75	58	91	89	74	65	60
One	32	40	42	47	58	48	46	36
Two	19	18	30	27	29	33	25	30
Three	17	5	9	11	7	6	9	3
Four or more	5	1	1	0	3	1	2	0
Total Left Back	73	64	82	85	97	88	82	69
Total Cases	167	139	140	176	186	162	147	129

With the exception of the fifth grades and the upper sixth, the mode expressing the frequency of non-promotion falls in the "one-time" group. The tendency of the pupils of Paterson who have reached the highest grades is to be left back once during their entire school life. Rather large percentages of pupils in all the grades of the grammar department, especially the high ones, are left back twice. In the lower grades a considerable number have repeated three times since they began school.

TABLE 26b

SAME CONVERTED TO PER CENT EQUIVALENTS

Left Back	5B	5A	6B	6A	7B	7A	8B	8A
	per cent	per cent	per cent	per cent	per cent	per cent	per cent	per cent
None	56	54	41	52	48	46	44	47
One	19	29	30	27	31	30	31	28
Two	11	13	21	15	16	20	17	23
Three	10	4	6	6	4	4	6	2
Four	3	1	1	0	2	1	1	0
Total Left Back	44	46	59	48	52	54	56	53

The statement showing the sex of the promoted and non-promoted children now in the grammar classes is found in the next tables. The graphic illustrations compare the boys and girls of the eighth grade as to relative frequency of promotion and repetition.

TABLE 27a

PUPILS REPEATING AND NON-REPEATING DURING SCHOOL LIFE

Boys in plain type. Girls in italics.

Left Back	5B	5A	6B	6A	7B	7A	8B	8A
None	*43* 51	*42* 33	*38* 20	*54* 37	*41* 48	*49* 25	*30* 35	*37* 23
One	*17* 15	*19* 21	*17* 25	*16* 31	*28* 30	*26* 22	*22* 24	*22* 14
Two	*6* 13	*14* 4	*11* 19	*16* 11	*12* 17	*21* 12	*12* 13	*11* 19
Three	*10* 7	*1* 4	*1* 8	*3* 8	*5* 2	*1* 5	*1* 8	*0* 3
Four	*1* 4	*1* 0	*0* 1	*0* 0	*1* 2	*0* 1	*0* 2	*0* 0
Total Left Back	*34* 39	*35* 29	*29* 53	*35* 50	*46* 51	*48* 40	*35* 47	*33* 36
Total Cases	*77* 90	*77* 62	*67* 73	*89* 87	*87* 99	*97* 65	*65* 82	*70* 59

TABLE 27b

SAME CONVERTED TO PER CENT EQUIVALENTS

Boys in plain type. Girls in italics.

Left Back	5B	5A	6B	6A	7B	7A	8B	8A	Average 8B and 8A
	per cent	per cent	per cent	per cent	per cent	per cent	per cent	per cent	per cent
None	*55.8* 56.7	*54.5* 53.2	*56.7* 27.4	*60.7* 42.5	*47.1* 48.5	*49.5* 38.5	*46.2* 42.7	*52.9* 39.0	*49.6* 41.1
One	*22.1* 16.7	*24.7* 33.9	*25.4* 34.2	*18.0* 35.6	*32.2* 30.3	*26.8* 33.8	*33.8* 29.3	*31.4* 23.7	*32.6* 27.0
Two	*7.8* 14.4	*18.2* 6.5	*16.4* 26.0	*18.0* 12.6	*13.8* 17.2	*21.6* 18.5	*18.5* 15.9	*15.7* 32.2	*17.0* 22.7
Three	*13.0* 7.8	*1.3* 6.5	*1.5* 11.0	*3.4* 9.2	*5.7* 2.0	*1.0* 7.7	*1.5* 9.8	*0.0* 5.1	*0.7* 7.8
Four	*1.3* 4.4	*1.3* 0.0	*0.0* 1.4	*0.0* 0.0	*1.1* 2.0	*0.0* 1.5	*0.0* 0.0	*0.0* 2.4	*0.0* 1.4
Total Left Back	*44.2* 43.3	*45.5* 46.8	*43.3* 72.6	*39.3* 57.5	*52.9* 51.5	*49.5* 61.5	*53.8* 57.3	*47.1* 61.0	*50.4* 58.9

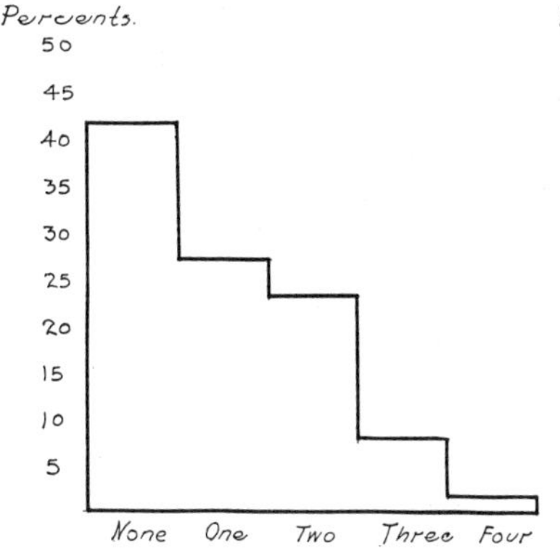

CHART 12 a. Eighth grade boys. Repeaters and non-repeaters during school life

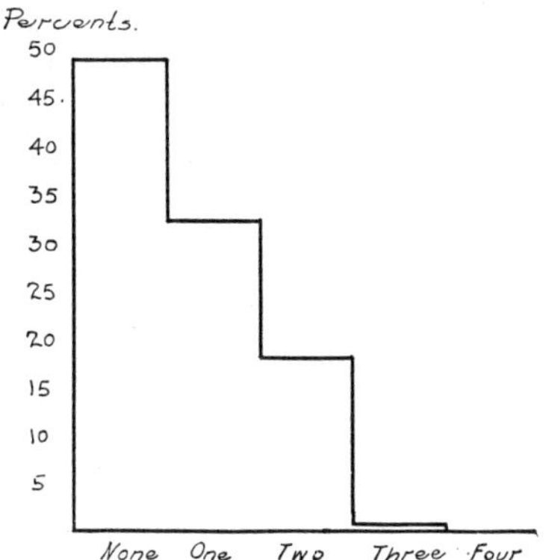

CHART 12 b. Eighth grade girls. Repeaters and non-repeaters during school life

From the bottom row of Table 27 b one notes that the boys fail to be promoted much more frequently than the girls in nearly all the grades. In the eighth grades whereas 49.6 per cent of the girls were never left back during their entire school life, the percentage in the case of the boys is 41.1. On the other hand, 50.4 per cent of the girls as opposed to 58.9 per cent of the boys were left back one or more times since their entrance in school.

The girls however show a greater tendency to be left back once, the boys being "held back" in larger numbers, two, three, and four times. In grades 5 B and 7 B the distribution is quite similar to that in the district of New York City reported in Chapter II, page 35. The boys may be placed here at both extremes of the distribution curve, the girls being about average. Measured then on the basis of the relative frequency of promotion and repetition, as read in all the grades tabulated, the girls of the Paterson schools are brighter than the boys. In Chart 12 a more variation is apparent than in Chart 12 b.

Tables 28 a and 28 b show again in numbers and in per cents respectively the relative frequency of non-promotion and the particular grades in which such non-promotion occurs.

TABLE 28a

GRADE DISTRIBUTION OF NON-PROMOTION IN AGGREGATE

Grades	8A	8B	7A	7B	6A	6B	5A	5B	4A	4B	3A	3B	2A	2B	1A	1B	Grand Total	
																	No. Left Back	Total Prom. and Non-prom.
8A	6	5	16	14	8	9	6	6	7	4	3	4	3	3	6	5	105	165
8B		10	17	10	7	12	7	14	11	9	5	10	3	8	4	4	131	196
7A			17	12	10	10	11	13	11	8	14	5	7	5	7	6	136	210
7B				24	15	12	18	14	13	11	5	11	7	7	8	4	149	238
6A					23	20	17	10	9	9	16	10	4	4	6	6	134	225
6B						23	12	15	14	8	12	14	7	12	8	9	134	192
5A							10	18	13	9	13	9	7	5	3	8	95	170
5B								26	17	9	17	14	19	11	16	12	141	235

Beginning with about three per cent as the average percentage of pupils now in the grammar grades who were left back in the first grades, there is a relatively steady increase from these grades till the eighth grades in the proportion of such non-promotions. The seventh grades in this system are unquestionably the selecting grades and those who are fortunate enough to withstand the strain here, proceed to the eighth grades where most all at the end of the "A" term are awarded the coveted diploma.

TABLE 28b

SAME IN PER CENTS

Using Total of Promoted and Non-Promoted as the Base

Grades	8A	8B	7A	7B	6A	6B	5A	5B	4A	4B	3A	3B	2A	2B	1A	1B
	per cent	per cent	per cent	per cent	per cent	per cent	per cent	per cent	per cent	per cent	per cent	per cent	per cent	per cent	per cent	per cent
8A	3.6	3.0	9.7	8.5	4.8	5.5	3.6	3.6	4.2	2.4	1.8	2.4	1.8	1.8	3.6	3.0
8B		5.1	8.7	5.1	3.6	6.1	3.6	7.1	5.6	4.6	2.5	5.1	1.5	4.1	2.0	2.0
7A			8.1	5.7	4.8	4.8	5.2	6.2	5.2	3.8	6.7	2.4	3.3	2.4	3.3	2.9
7B				10.1	6.3	5.0	7.6	5.9	5.5	4.6	2.1	4.6	2.9	2.9	3.4	1.7
6A					10.2	8.9	7.6	4.4	4.0	4.0	7.1	4.4	1.8	1.8	2.6	2.6
6B						12.0	6.2	7.8	7.3	4.2	6.2	7.3	3.6	6.2	4.2	4.7
5A							5.9	10.6	7.6	5.3	7.6	5.3	4.1	2.9	1.8	4.7
5B								11.0	7.2	3.8	7.2	6.0	8.1	4.7	6.8	5.1
Aver.	3.6	4.2	8.8	7.4	6.1	7.0	5.8	7.1	5.8	4.1	5.2	4.7	3.5	3.4	3.6	3.3

Proceeding as in the previous chapters to a brief comparative study of grade retention, the failures in the 3 A and 3 B grades of the present 7 A and 7 B pupils as compared with the present 5 A and 5 B pupils may be gleaned from Table 28 b.

GRADES....	3A per cent	3B per cent
In 7A grade..........	6.7	2.4
In 7B grade..........	2.1	4.6
Median...........	3.5	

GRADES....	3A per cent	3B per cent
In 5A grade.........	7.6	5.3
In 5B grade.........	7.2	6.0
Median...........	6.6	

In the fifth grades about 1 in 15 was left back in the third grades. Of the present seventh grade pupils approximately 1 in 30 failed in these grades.

Comparing now the eighth and seventh grades with the sixth and fifth grades on the basis of failure of promotion in the third grades the following may be noted:

GRADES....	3A per cent	3B per cent
In 8A grade..........	1.8	2.4
In 8B grade..........	2.5	5.1
In 7A grade..........	6.7	2.4
In 7B grade..........	2.1	4.6
Median...........	2.45	

GRADES....	3A per cent	3B per cent
In 6A grade.........	7.1	4.4
In 6B grade.........	6.2	7.3
In 5A grade.........	7.6	5.3
In 5B grade.........	7.2	6.0
Median...........	6.65	

The chance then that a sixth grade or a fifth grade pupil was left back in the third grade is more than twice as great as is the case of a pupil known to have reached the seventh or the eighth grade. Only 1 in 40 of these upper grade grammar pupils repeated the primary grade in question; whereas the ratio of retention in the case of the fifth and the sixth grade pupils is about 1 to 15.

Taking the averages of the "A" and "B" grades to count as the amount of retention in what would be a single yearly grade, the percentages are as follows:

GRADES:	First	Second	Third	Fourth	Fifth	Sixth	Seventh	Eighth
	3.4	3.4	5.0	5.0	6.5	6.6	8.0	4.0

In no other city system is the steady gradual increase from the first till the eighth grade so marked as in the Paterson schools.

CHAPTER V

EAST ORANGE, N. J. 448 CASES

The selection of the East Orange schools for study was prompted by the desire to get records from enough select schools to offset those obtained from the schools of the other cities attended largely by the poorer class of children. Only four schools in East Orange have the complete graded system extending through the grammar department. They have an approximate register of 500, 600, 550, 650 pupils, respectively. These schools were visited in March and April, 1910.

THE MIGRATION OF PUPILS

Small percentages of initial starters characterize the condition in the East Orange system. This is a result of the combined action of three main causes: the considerable migration from school to school in the city itself, also from other cities, and the tendency of the parents to send their children in their earlier years to private institutions with a view to have them transferred later to the regular public schools.

TABLE 29

PER CENTS OF INITIAL STARTERS

Schools	Q	R	S	T	Average
Grades	per cent	per cent	per cent	per cent	per cent
Eighth	36	43	43	34	39.9
Seventh	33	38	24	41	33.8
Sixth	42	33	31	26	30.4
Fifth	38	33	38	66	43.3
Fourth	52	36	53	42	45.7
Average	40	37	38	42	38.3

Only 38.3 per cent of those who are now in grades four to eight inclusive originally entered the schools in which they now attend. Although the larger percentages are apparent in the fourth and fifth grades this does not signify that the migratory tendency is becoming less active. Many of these lower grade initial starters will be eliminated in, or perhaps before, they reach the higher grades, and so these percentages will be reduced to at least the same level as those now recorded in the upper three classes.

The Age-Grade Relations of the 448 Initial Starters

In the following age-grade table the grammar grade pupils including those in the fourth grade are distributed according to their age at the time of entrance to their present grade.

TABLE 30

Four Schools. Age Distribution. Aggregate 448 Cases

Grades	9	10	11	12	13	14	15	16	17	Total	Above Normal Age	
											No.	Per cent
Eighth				5	19	40	26	12	3	105	81	77.1
Seventh			6	9	25	22	11	1		74	59	79.3
Sixth			12	13	15	15	2			57	45	78.9
Fifth	1	14	35	22	9	10				91	76	83.5
Fourth	23	35	31	22	10					121	98	81.0
							Total.......			448	Cases	

From Table 30 one notes in the last column the percentages of "over-ageness" in the five grades. These figures are surprisingly high. The lower grades seem especially burdened with retarded pupils. Assuming 9 years to 9 years 11 months inclusive as the normal entrance age to the fourth grade, 81 per cent of the initial starters in this grade in the four schools are "over-age."

In the fifth grade adding one year to the theoretical age limit assumed in the fourth grade, a still larger proportion of pupils are above the normal age.

More pupils 16 and 17 years of age are found in the graduating classes of these "aristocratic" schools than in the schools of the cities previously treated. It is evident that the parents can afford to permit their children to remain in school until they finish, no matter how long it takes them to accomplish the course. The same is likewise noticeable in the select schools of Plainfield, considered in the next chapter.

Taking 10 years to 10 years 11 months as the normal age for the fourth grade, 11 years to 11 years 11 months, for the fifth grade, etc., these percentages of retarded pupils reduce as follows: Eighth grade, 39.0 per cent; sixth grade, 56.1 per cent; fifth grade, 45.1 per cent; fourth grade, 52.1 per cent.

Distributing these retarded pupils according to sex, Table 31 and Charts 13 a and 13 b show the desired comparison.

TABLE 31

FOUR SCHOOLS. AGE-GRADE TABLE SHOWING SEX DISTRIBUTION

Boys in plain type. Girls in italics.

Grades	9	10	11	12	13	14	15	16	17	Total	Above Normal Age	
											No.	Per cent
Eighth				*2* 3	*10* 9	*17* 23	*16* 10	*7* 5	*1* 2	*53* 52	*41* 40	*77.4* 76.9
Seventh			*3* 3	*7* 2	*17* 8	*10* 12	*7* 4	*0* 1		*44* 30	*34* 25	*77.3* 83.3
Sixth			*6* 6	*9* 4	*7* 8	*7* 8	*0* 2			*29* 28	*23* 22	*79.3* 78.6
Fifth	*0* 1	*9* 5	*18* 17	*7* 15	*4* 5	*1* 9				*39* 52	*30* 46	*76.9* 88.5
Fourth	*17* 6	*16* 19	*14* 17	*6* 16	*3* 7					*56* 65	*39* 59	*69.6* 90.8
						Total...........				*221* 227	Girls Boys	

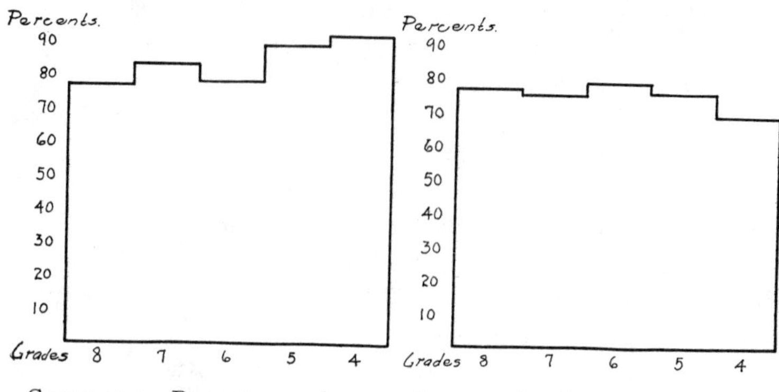

CHART 13 a. Percentages of retarded boys

CHART 13 b. Percentages of retarded girls

The median percentage above normal age in the case of the boys is in the seventh grade, 83.3 per cent. In the case of the girls it is also found in the same grade with 77.3 per cent retarded. The boys are much more retarded than the girls in the fourth, fifth, and seventh grades of this system. In the other two grades, the ratios are about equal. The percentages of "over-age" boys as compared with the girls in the seventh and eighth grades reduce in greater proportion when the age limit is extended in these grades up to 14 years and up to 15 years respectively.

The graphic illustrations following Table 31 show the considerable variability manifested by the retarded boys as against the

TABLE 32

AGE DISTRIBUTION OF 448 PUPILS AT TIME OF ENTRANCE TO THE FIRST GRADE

Schools	5	6	7	8	9	Total	Above Normal Age	
							No.	Per cent
Q	13	47	28	9	1	98	38	38.8
R	29	52	32	7	1	121	40	33.1
S	20	49	32	14	0	115	46	40.0
T	20	53	38	2	1	114	41	35.9
Total	82	201	130	32	3	448	165	36.8

comparatively even distribution of the "over-age" girls in grades four through eight.

Table 32 is a statement of the ages of the 448 pupils when they entered school.

Only 36.8 per cent of the 448 pupils whose records were taken were seven years or more when they entered the first school grade. The six-year column evidently in all the four schools holds the modal entrance group. The schools are seen to vary only slightly in the matter of "over-age" initial starters, the median being approximately 37 per cent.

The distribution of pupils with respect to school, present grade, and initial entrance age is shown in the next table.

In this table showing the age-grade groups of the initial starters one notes that whereas the largest percentages of present grade "over-ageness" as read in Table 30 are recorded in the fourth and fifth grades, here too the minimum and maximum amounts are registered as above the assumed normal age for these same grades. Again the reader is cautioned not to take these latter percentages in certain explanation of the former. Although the groups treated are the same, the individuals who were "over-age" may be by no means the same individuals who were "over-age" in their present grades. Comparing Tables 32 and 33 there seems to be more evidence of deviation from the median percentage above normal age in the five grades in the latter, where the pupils are distributed according to grades, than in the former table wherein merely school totals are recorded.

Relative sex comparisons of the ages of the initial starters when they entered school follow on pages 73 and 74. The appended diagrams compare only those boys and girls who were above 6 years 11 months when they were admitted to the first grade.

The percentage of boys now in the grammar and fourth grades who were "over-age" on admission to the first grade is a trifle more than the corresponding percentage of girls. In the one case it is 37.9 per cent; in the other, 35.7 per cent. The boys at present are retarded in great numbers in the fourth grade (see Table 31). From Table 34 it appears that a very small percentage of these fourth grade boys were "over-age" when they entered school. In the fifth grade, however, whereas 88.5

TABLE 33

AGE GRADE DISTRIBUTION OF 448 PUPILS AT TIME OF ENTRANCE TO FIRST GRADE

Ages	Five Years				Six Years				Seven Years				Eight Years				Nine Years				Total Cases	Above Normal Age	
Schools	Q	R	S	T	Q	R	S	T	Q	R	S	T	Q	R	S	T	Q	R	S	T		No.	Per cent
Grades																							
Eighth	4	4	5	2	11	15	14	10	5	14	6	3	1	5	5	0	0	1	0	0	105	40	38.1
Seventh	2	7	3	1	6	9	9	9	9	4	0	10	1	1	1	2	0	0	0	0	74	28	37.8
Sixth	0	5	4	3	4	4	8	6	1	6	7	7	0	0	2	0	0	0	0	0	57	23	40.3
Fifth	3	3	1	4	8	14	1	11	5	5	10	17	6	0	1	0	1	0	0	1	91	46	50.5
Fourth	4	10	7	10	18	10	17	17	8	3	9	1	1	1	5	0	0	0	0	0	121	28	23.1
Total	13	29	20	20	47	52	49	53	28	32	32	38	9	7	14	2	1	1	0	1	448	165	36.8

TABLE 34

AGE-GRADE SEX DISTRIBUTION OF 448 PUPILS AT TIME OF ENTRANCE TO FIRST GRADE

Boys in plain type. Girls in italics.

Ages	Five Years				Six Years				Seven Years				Eight Years				Nine Years				Total Cases	Above Normal Age	
Schools	Q	R	S	T	Q	R	S	T	Q	R	S	T	Q	R	S	T	Q	R	S	T		No.	Percent
Grades Eighth	*2*	*1*	*1*	*2*	*7*	*9*	*6*	*6*	*3*	*6*	*5*	*2*	*0*	*2*	*1*	*0*	*0*	*0*	*0*	*0*	*53*	*19*	*35.8*
	2	3	4	0	4	6	8	4	2	8	1	1	1	3	4	0	0	1	0	0	52	21	40.4
Seventh	*1*	*3*	*2*	*0*	*4*	*4*	*7*	*6*	*5*	*3*	*0*	*5*	*1*	*0*	*1*	*2*	*0*	*0*	*0*	*0*	*44*	*17*	*38.6*
	1	4	1	1	2	5	2	3	4	1	0	5	0	1	0	0	0	0	0	0	30	11	36.7
Sixth	*0*	*2*	*1*	*2*	*3*	*2*	*1*	*4*	*0*	*3*	*4*	*5*	*0*	*0*	*2*	*0*	*0*	*0*	*0*	*0*	*29*	*14*	*48.3*
	0	3	3	1	1	2	7	2	1	3	3	2	0	0	0	0	0	0	0	0	28	9	32.1
Fifth	*1*	*1*	*1*	*2*	*3*	*5*	*1*	*8*	*1*	*3*	*3*	*7*	*1*	*0*	*1*	*0*	*0*	*0*	*0*	*1*	*39*	*17*	*43.6*
	2	2	0	2	5	9	0	3	4	2	7	10	5	0	0	0	1	0	0	0	52	29	55.8
Fourth	*3*	*4*	*4*	*4*	*5*	*3*	*9*	*12*	*4*	*3*	*5*	*0*	*0*	*0*	*0*	*0*	*0*	*0*	*0*	*0*	*56*	*12*	*21.4*
	1	6	3	6	13	7	8	5	4	0	4	1	1	1	5	0	0	0	0	0	65	16	24.6
Total	*7*	*11*	*9*	*10*	*22*	*23*	*24*	*36*	*13*	*18*	*17*	*19*	*2*	*2*	*5*	*2*	*0*	*0*	*0*	*1*	*221*	*79*	*35.7*
	6	18	11	10	25	29	25	17	15	14	15	19	7	5	9	0	1	1	0	0	227	86	37.9

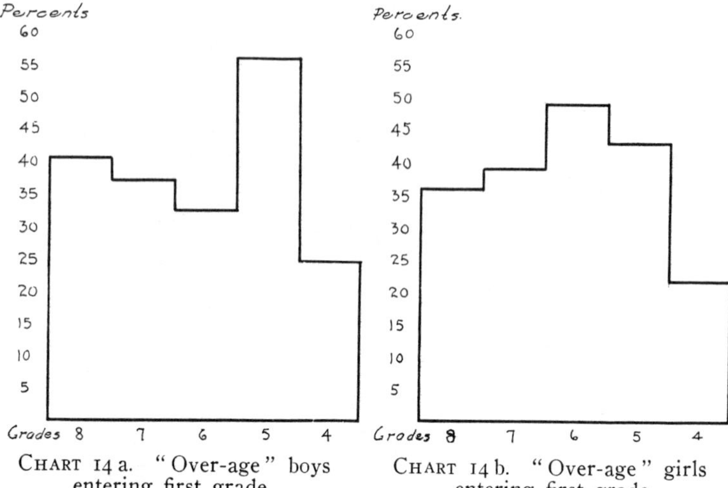

CHART 14 a. "Over-age" boys entering first grade

CHART 14 b. "Over-age" girls entering first grade.

per cent of the boys are at present retarded, 55.8 per cent of this same group of boys were "over-age" in the first grade. The percentages of "over-age" girls of the sixth and seventh grades are larger than is the case with the boys in these same grades. In the other grades the reverse is true. The records for all the grades show the boys to be more variable than the girls.

THE INCIDENCE OF RETARDATION

The following tables outline the repeaters and non-repeaters during their entire school life with respect to present grade distribution. Table 35 a records the actual numbers of promoted and non-promoted children; Table 35 b, the per cents.

TABLE 35a

FOUR SCHOOLS. AGGREGATE 448 CASES

Left Back	Fourth	Fifth	Sixth	Seventh	Eighth
None	71	56	35	43	66
One	28	28	15	26	30
Two	20	7	6	5	9
Three	2	0	1	0	0
Total Left Back	50	35	22	31	39
Total Cases	121	91	57	74	105

TABLE 35b

Same Converted to Per Cent Equivalents

Left Back	Fourth	Fifth	Sixth	Seventh	Eighth
	per cent	per cent	per cent	per cent	per cent
None	59	62	61	58	63
One	23	31	26	35	29
Two	17	8	11	7	9
Three	2	0	2	0	0
Total Left Back	41	38	39	42	37

In East Orange a rather anomalous situation presents itself. Table 30 proves the excessive extent of retardation in the schools studied. Table 33 shows a relatively small amount of "over-ageness" of these initial starters at the time of their entrance to the first grade. Finally, Table 35 b to perplex the problem records exceedingly high percentages of regular promotion: 59 per cent in the fourth grade; 62 per cent in the fifth; 61 per cent in the sixth; 58 per cent in the seventh; and 63 per cent in the eighth. In each case the mode falls in the uppermost row. In the fifth grade where retardation registered a maximum of 83.5 per cent, the percentage of pupils never left back (Table 35 b) is 62 per cent; with 31 per cent repeating once, and 8 per cent, twice. A possible explanation of this exceptional condition would be found in complete age-grade tables for the school year 1909-10. Unfortunately no such tables are published in any of the superintendent's reports.

The regularly promoted boys and girls and those repeating once, twice, and three times throughout the entire school course are distributed in Tables 36 a and 36 b.

Table 36 b states that 58.5 per cent of the 53 girls reported in the eighth grade were promoted regularly since their entrance in school; 34 per cent were left back once; and 7.5 per cent, twice. Of the 52 eighth grade boys, 67.3 per cent were never left back; 23.1 per cent repeated once; and 9.6 per cent, twice, during their entire school life.

Thus measured the boys show a greater range of mental ability than the girls, the latter occupying the average position; the former, the two extremes of the normal distributory curve. (See Charts 15 a and 15 b.)

In grades 4, 5, 6, and 7, however, the girls show by far larger percentages of regular promotion, than the boys. Reading from

TABLE 36a

PUPILS REPEATING AND NON-REPEATING DURING ENTIRE SCHOOL LIFE

Boys in plain type. Girls in italics.

Left Back	Fourth	Fifth	Sixth	Seventh	Eighth
None	*37* 34	*27* 29	*20* 15	*30* 13	*31* 35
One	*10* 18	*11* 17	*7* 8	*11* 15	*18* 12
Two	*9* 11	*1* 6	*1* 5	*3* 2	*4* 5
Three	*0* 2	*0* 0	*1* 0	*0* 0	*0* 0
Total Left Back	*19* 31	*12* 23	*9* 13	*14* 17	*22* 17
Total Cases	*56* 65	*39* 52	*29* 28	*44* 30	*53* 52

TABLE 36b

SAME CONVERTED TO PER CENT EQUIVALENTS

Boys in plain type. Girls in italics.

Left Back	Fourth	Fifth	Sixth	Seventh	Eighth
	per cent	per cent	per cent	per cent	per cent
None	*66.1* 52.3	*69.2* 55.8	*69.0* 53.6	*68.2* 43.3	*58.5* 67.3
One	*17.9* 27.7	*28.2* 32.7	*24.1* 28.6	*25.0* 50.0	*34.0* 23.1
Two	*16.1* 16.9	*2.6* 11.5	*3.4* 17.9	*6.8* 6.7	*7.5* 9.6
Three	*0.0* 3.1	*0.0* 0.0	*3.4* 0.0	*0.0* 0.0	*0.0* 0.0
Total Left Back	*33.9* 47.7	*30.8* 44.2	*31.0* 46.4	*31.8* 56.7	*41.5* 32.7

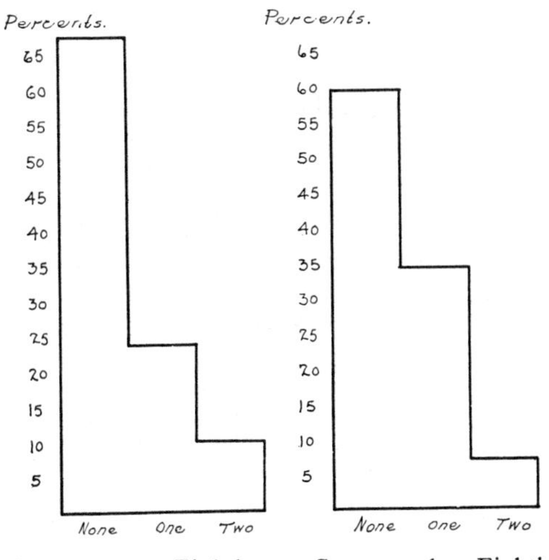

CHART 15 a. Eighth grade boys. CHART 15 b. Eighth grade girls.

Repeaters and non-repeaters during school life

the bottom row of Table 36 b one notes that in all grades excepting the highest the boys repeat much oftener than the girls.

The grade distributions of the repeaters in the grammar and fourth grades of the East Orange schools (Tables 37 a and 37 b) show the relative frequencies in number and per cent respectively.

TABLE 37a

GRADE DISTRIBUTION OF NON-PROMOTION IN AGGREGATE

Grades	Eighth	Seventh	Sixth	Fifth	Fourth	Third	Second	First	Grand Total	
									No. Left Back	Total Prom. and Non-Prom.
Eighth	5	17	8	5	5	3	1	4	48	114
Seventh		9	6	7	5	2	3	4	36	79
Sixth			9	5	3	4	4	5	30	65
Fifth				10	7	7	10	8	42	98
Fourth					17	22	16	19	74	145

TABLE 37b

SAME IN PER CENTS

Using Total of Promoted and Non-Promoted as the Base

Grades	Eighth	Seventh	Sixth	Fifth	Fourth	Third	Second	First
	per cent	per cent	per cent	per cent	per cent	per cent	per cent	per cent
Eighth	4.4	14.9	7.0	4.4	4.4	2.6	0.9	3.5
Seventh		11.4	7.6	8.9	6.3	2.5	3.8	5.1
Sixth			13.8	7.7	4.6	6.2	6.2	7.7
Fifth				10.2	7.2	7.2	10.2	8.2
Fourth					11.7	15.2	11.0	13.1
Aver.	4.4	13.5	8.9	7.6	7.4	7.6	6.8	8.0

From the averages obtained, with due regard to the proper totals of promoted and non-promoted in grades 4 to 8 inclusive, one learns that the seventh grade holds clearly the maximum record of retention. Eliminating the first grade, the grades from the second till the eighth increase in percentages of "hold-overs," progressively to the seventh, in which grade an amazingly large percentage of non-promotion is recorded. A considerable drop quite as remarkable is manifest in the final grade. Unquestionably in this small city school system the seventh grade is the potent selective force in deciding on the competent ones fitted to enter the graduating class.

Taken from Table 37 b the following percentages compare grade retention:

	THIRD GRADE per cent
In eighth grade	2.6
In sixth grade	6.2
In fourth grade	15.2

Whereas 1 pupil in 38 of those now in the eighth grade was left back in the third grade, for those in the sixth grade the ratio is 1 to 16 and for those in the fourth grade about 1 to 7.

Again comparing those now in the eighth and the seventh grades who were left back in the third grade, with those now in the fifth and the fourth grades, the distribution is as follows:

	THIRD GRADE per cent
In eighth grade.....	2.6
In seventh grade...	2.5
Median..........	2.55

	THIRD GRADE per cent
In fifth grade......	7.2
In fourth grade....	15.2
Median.........	11.2

The probable chance then that a fifth or a fourth grade pupil was left back in the third grade is at least four times as great as in the case of the eighth or the seventh grade pupil.

The indication from Table 37 b that in the grammar grades excepting the graduating class, the pupils are invariably retained more frequently in their present grade than in the previous grades is evidence that a gradual eliminating process is at work in grades five and on, culminating in the difficult seventh. In this grade so much pressure is brought to bear on the pupils that about every seventh one is forced to repeat or suffer elimination.

CHAPTER VI

PLAINFIELD, N. J. 485 CASES

The Plainfield system is distinctive in that it segregates the sixth, seventh, and eighth year pupils in central schools. The lower grades are distributed regularly in the other schools. The tables in this chapter show then the distributions with respect to grade only.

The city of Plainfield was included in this special study because it was the only system situated within convenient distance of New York City in which complete history cards were obtainable. These individual record-forms of the pupils dating back to the time when they entered the first grade of the school show accurately the regular promotions and the incidence of grade repetition. The writer, however, visited each class room of the fifth, sixth, seventh, and eighth grades and questioned the pupils individually as in the other cities. Their written answers were then carefully checked up by the official record cards and the errors corrected. It is significant to mention here, this being the one city wherein it was possible to check up all the records, that the pupils made comparatively few mistakes in answering the formal questions. Such errors as were found, were mostly in reply to the question asking the pupils to state the number of times they were left back during their entire school life and the grades in which they were retained. The fact is that in nearly every case where the individuals' own statements were unwittingly false concerning the latter in particular, their memory seemed to waver only in the case of the primary grades. Quite often the pupil himself when in doubt as to his failure in an upper grade was reminded either by his classmates or perhaps by the teacher.

Again, wherever it was found that the pupils deliberately misstated the facts, their records as read from the individual history cards were invariably somewhat worse than they cared to admit. For example, when pupils replied that they were left back a given number of times, on checking up their statements it was found that in no case were they left back less than they stated. On the other hand, in quite a number of instances their history cards showed one or more retentions above the number admitted by them in class.

The Migration of Pupils

The per cents of initial starters are distributed as follows in the grammar grades of the Plainfield schools:

TABLE 38

Per Cents of Initial Starters

	Eighth	Seventh	Sixth	Fifth	Average
Grammar Grades	per cent	per cent	per cent	per cent	per cent
	56	53	57	56	56

The percentages in Table 38 are high when compared with those of the other four cities because of the prevailing method of centralizing the upper grade pupils as previously explained. All those pupils who entered the first grade of any public school in Plainfield proper were recorded in this particular city; whereas in the other cities only those who entered the first grade of the school in which they now attend or in its official "feeding" school were rated as initial starters and their records sought. From Table 38 one reads that 56 per cent of the pupils now in the grammar grades of the Plainfield schools entered the first grade of one of the schools in that city.

The Age-Grade Relations of the 485 Initial Starters

The ages of the 485 pupils when they entered their present grades are given in Table 39.

Assuming 10 years to 10 years 11 months inclusive as the normal entrance age to the fifth grade; 11 years to 11 years 11 months inclusive for the sixth grade, etc., the percentages of "over-age" grammar grade pupils are shown in the last column of Table 39. The largest proportion of retarded pupils is found in the eighth grade. The percentages in all four grades are rather high.

TABLE 39

GRAMMAR GRADES. AGE DISTRIBUTION. AGGREGATE 485 CASES

Grades	9	10	11	12	13	14	15	16	17	18	Total	Above Normal Age	
												No.	Per cent
Eighth				1	17	29	21	13	3	1	85	67	78.8
Seventh			5	37	36	32	12	5	1		128	86	67.2
Sixth	1	2	36	59	34	22	2	1			157	118	75.2
Fifth	6	25	35	19	21	5	4				115	84	73.0
										Total.......	485	Cases	

Counting only those as retarded who exceed the assumed normal age by one or more years in the respective grades the proportion of "over-age" pupils would be: Eighth grade, 44.7 per cent; seventh grade, 39.1 per cent; sixth grade, 37.6 per cent; fifth grade, 42.6 per cent.

The sex distribution of the 485 initial starters respecting age-grade relations is to be noted in the following table and graphic illustrations:

TABLE 40

GRAMMAR GRADES. AGE-GRADE TABLE SHOWING SEX DISTRIBUTION

Boys in plain type. Girls in italics.

Grades	9	10	11	12	13	14	15	16	17	18	Total	Above Normal Age	
												No.	Per cent
Eighth				*1* 0	*10* 7	*13* 16	*13* 8	*7* 6	*2* 1	*1* 0	*47* 38	*36* 31	*76.6* 81.6
Seventh			*2* 3	*21* 16	*13* 23	*15* 17	*6* 6	*3* 2	*0* 1		*60* 68	*37* 49	*61.7* 72.1
Sixth	*0* 1	*2* 0	*11* 25	*31* 28	*17* 17	*9* 13	*0* 2	*1* 0			*71* 86	*58* 60	*81.7* 69.8
Fifth	*3* 3	*13* 12	*13* 22	*10* 9	*8* 13	*1* 4	*1* 3				*49* 66	*33* 51	*67.3* 77.3
										Total.......	*227* 258	Girls Boys	

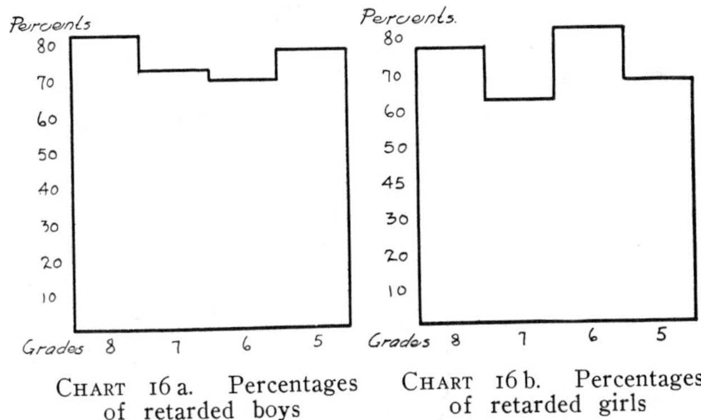

CHART 16 a. Percentages of retarded boys

CHART 16 b. Percentages of retarded girls

The boys in grades eight, seven, and five are more retarded than the girls. Whereas in the sixth grade 81.7 per cent of the girls are "over-age," the boys record only 69.8 per cent. Allowing one year on the assumed theoretical age-limit for this grade, these percentages would change to 38.0 per cent in the case of the girls and to 37.2 per cent for the boys. The modal age for the fifth grade girls and boys is evidently 11 years to 11 years 11 months inclusive; for the sixth grade, 12 years to 12 years 11 months inclusive, etc. Assuming these age-limits the girls show 40.4 per cent with an average deviation of 2.95 as the median percentage of retardation for the four grades, the median for the boys being 38.85 per cent, A. D. 2.0. The girls of the grammar grades in this school system are more variable than the boys in the matter of present "over-ageness."

TABLE 41

AGE DISTRIBUTION OF 485 PUPILS AT TIME OF ENTRANCE TO FIRST GRADE

Ages	4	5	6	7	8	9	10	Total	Above Normal Age	
									No.	Per cent
Grammar Grades	2	79	249	111	29	12	3	485	155	32.0

The 485 pupils entering the initial grade in any of the Plainfield schools are distributed in the above table according to their ages at the time of such entrance. One hundred and fifty-five of these children or 32 per cent were "over-age" when they began school. The modal entrance age is clearly 6 years 0 months to 6 years 11 months inclusive.

The next table records the age-grade distribution of these initial starters classified according to present grade.

TABLE 42

AGE-GRADE DISTRIBUTION OF 485 PUPILS AT TIME OF ENTRANCE TO FIRST GRADE

Ages	4	5	6	7	8	9	10	Total	Above Normal Age	
									No.	Per cent
Grades										
Eighth	1	24	35	19	5	1	0	85	25	29.4
Seventh	0	32	66	24	3	3	0	128	30	23.4
Sixth	1	12	93	36	13	2	0	157	51	32.5
Fifth	0	11	55	32	8	6	3	115	49	42.6
Total	2	79	249	111	29	12	3	485	155	32.0

The lower grammar grades show considerably more initial "over-ageness" than the upper grades. From Table 39 one notes that the percentages of retardation at present in the two lower as compared with the two higher classes approximately average the same.

The classification in the following age-grade table (Table 43) shows the sex distribution of the initial starters.

Of the 258 boys whose records were taken in Plainfield, 78 or 30.2 per cent were seven years or more when they entered the first grade; whereas of the 227 girls 77 or 33.9 per cent were above normal age at that time. In the eighth grade and especially in the fifth grade the girls show more initial "over-ageness" than the boys. Concerning the percentages of present grade retardation as read in Table 40, the boys in both fifth and eighth grades record the larger proportions. The greater variability among the girls as illustrated in Charts 16 a and 16 b is perhaps a result of the similar tendency manifest at school entrance.

TABLE 43

AGE-GRADE SEX DISTRIBUTION OF 485 PUPILS AT TIME OF ENTRANCE TO FIRST GRADE

Boys in plain type. Girls in italics.

Ages	4	5	6	7	8	9	10	Total	Above Normal Age: No.	Above Normal Age: Per cent
Grades Eighth	*1* 0	*12* 12	*19* 16	*13* 6	*2* 3	*0* 1	*0* 0	*47* 38	*15* 10	*31.9* 26.3
Seventh	*0* 0	*16* 16	*31* 35	*10* 14	*1* 2	*2* 1	*0* 0	*60* 68	*13* 17	*21.7* 25.0
Sixth	*0* 1	*6* 6	*42* 51	*17* 19	*6* 7	*0* 2	*0* 0	*71* 86	*23* 28	*32.4* 32.6
Fifth	*0* 0	*3* 8	*20* 35	*19* 13	*4* 4	*2* 4	*1* 2	*49* 66	*26* 23	*53.1* 34.8
Total	*1* 1	*37* 42	*112* 137	*59* 52	*13* 16	*4* 8	*1* 2	*227* 258	*77* 78	*33.9* 30.2

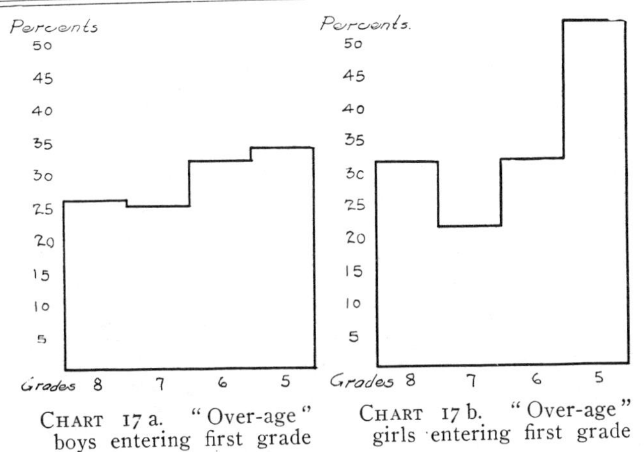

CHART 17 a. "Over-age" boys entering first grade

CHART 17 b. "Over-age" girls entering first grade

THE INCIDENCE OF RETARDATION

Tables 44 a and 44 b indicate in aggregate and in per cent respectively the present grade distribution of repeaters.

It appears from Tables 44 a and 44 b that of the 85 eighth grade pupils recorded, only 9 per cent were never left back during their entire school life; 48 per cent were left back once; 32 per cent twice; and 10 per cent three times. These extraordinary percentages need explanation. Until four years ago the Plainfield schools had in reality though not officially a nine year system. Children entered a so-called lower first class, remained there a year, and then advanced to the upper first class, a yearly grade also. Only the exceptionally bright were permitted to advance to the second grade after spending one year in the initial grade. This arrangement was abolished quite recently. The records, however, of the present grammar grade pupils are af-

TABLE 44a

GRAMMAR GRADES. AGGREGATE 485 CASES

Left Back	Fifth	Sixth	Seventh	Eighth
None	32	44	25	8
One	51	59	52	41
Two	22	38	31	27
Three	9	14	13	9
Four	1	1	6	0
Five	0	1	1	0
Total Left Back	83	113	103	77
Total Cases	115	157	128	85

TABLE 44b

SAME CONVERTED TO PER CENT EQUIVALENTS

Left Back	Fifth	Sixth	Seventh	Eighth
	per cent	per cent	per cent	per cent
None	28	28	20	9
One	44	38	41	48
Two	19	24	24	32
Three	8	9	10	10
Four	1	1	5	0
Five	0	1	1	0
Total Left Back	72	72	80	91

fected in consequence. The superintendent now insists that the teachers record all the pupils who remained in the first grade more than one year as having repeated that grade. Advancement from lower to upper first grade is not regarded as a promotion in such cases where the pupil remained over a year in these classes. In the majority of cases when the writer checked up the records of the pupils who claimed not to have been left back since school entrance, it was found that the history cards reported a non-promotion in the first grade. These latter records being officially sanctioned by the superintendent it was thought best to employ them rather than those gathered in the class rooms from the pupils. Naturally in all the grammar grades one notes that the tendency of non-promotion during school life is recorded in the "one-time" group. In all probability eliminating the first grade repeaters the mode would fall in the top row.

Classifying the repeaters and non-repeaters according to sex, the following tables and charts show the distributions:

TABLE 45a

Pupils Repeating and Non-Repeating During School Life

Boys in plain type. Girls in italics.

Left Back	Fifth	Sixth	Seventh	Eighth
None	*16* 16	*24* 20	*12* 13	*5* 3
One	*22* 29	*24* 35	*23* 29	*21* 20
Two	*8* 14	*13* 25	*17* 14	*15* 12
Three	*3* 6	*9* 5	*6* 7	*6* 3
Four	*0* 1	*1* 0	*1* 5	*0* 0
Five	*0* 0	*0* 1	*1* 0	*0* 0
Total Left Back	*33* 53	*47* 66	*48* 55	*42* 35
Total Cases	*49* 66	*71* 86	*60* 68	*47* 38

TABLE 45b

SAME CONVERTED TO PER CENT EQUIVALENTS

Boys in plain type. Girls in italics.

Left Back	Fifth	Sixth	Seventh	Eighth
	per cent	per cent	per cent	per cent
None	*32.7* 24.2	*33.8* 23.3	*20.0* 19.1	*10.6* 7.9
One	*44.9* 43.9	*33.8* 40.7	*38.3* 42.6	*44.7* 52.6
Two	*16.5* 21.2	*18.3* 29.1	*28.3* 20.6	*31.9* 31.6
Three	*6.1* 9.1	*12.7* 5.8	*10.0* 10.3	*12.8* 7.9
Four	*0.0* 1.5	*1.4* 0.0	*1.7* 7.4	*0.0* 0.0
Five	*0.0* 0.0	*0.0* 1.2	*1.7* 0.0	*0.0* 0.0
Total Left Back	*67.3* 80.3	*66.2* 76.7	*80.0* 80.9	*89.4* 92.1

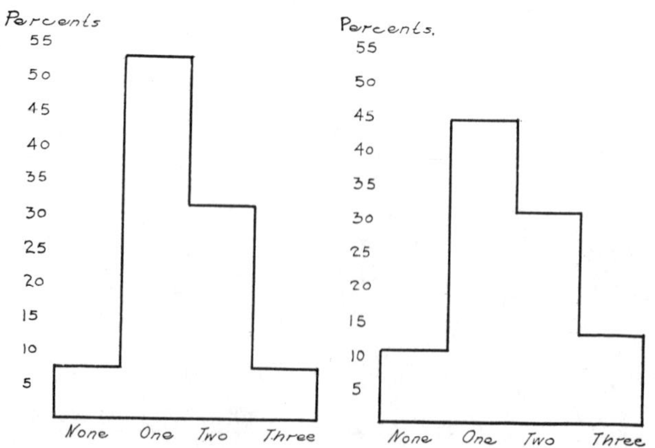

CHART 18 a. Eighth grade boys. Repeaters and non-repeaters during school life

CHART 18 b. Eighth grade girls. Repeaters and non-repeaters during school life

The eighth grade girls of the Plainfield schools show at once better records of regular promotion and the larger percentages of more frequent repetition.

The boys and girls indicate a modal tendency of repeating once during their entire school life. In the matter of frequency of non-promotion, the boys are more variable than the girls. (Compare Charts 18 a and 18 b.)

In all the grammar grades the following is noted: That the girls are more often regularly promoted; that the girls are less frequently held back once, the median in the case of the girls in the "one-time" row being 41.5 per cent, in the case of the boys, 43.3 per cent; that the girls repeat less often twice, and more often three times. The few repeaters four and five times do not justify sex comparison.

The results of the early system of grading previously explained are shown plainly in the next two tables outlining the incidence of retardation of those repeaters who are now in the central schools including the fifth grade pupils.

TABLE 46a

GRADE DISTRIBUTION OF NON-PROMOTION IN AGGREGATE

Grades	Eighth	Seventh	Sixth	Fifth	Fourth	Third	Second	First	Grand Total	
									No. Left Back	Total Prom. and Non-prom.
Eighth	4	26	14	13	7	8	10	40	122	130
Seventh		29	38	15	14	11	13	62	182	207
Sixth			37	24	20	15	16	74	186	230
Fifth				24	21	10	9	62	126	158

Reading from the right in the bottom row of Table 46 b (page 90), 32.8 per cent of the total promoted and non-promoted grammar grade pupils were left back in the first grade; 6.6 per cent in the second grade; 6.1 per cent in the third; 8.6 per cent in the fourth; 10.5 per cent in the fifth; 15.7 per cent in the sixth; 16.3 per cent in the seventh; and 3.1 per cent in the eighth. These figures, not considering the first grade, indicate a progressive increase from the second grade through the seventh. The sixth grade school would seem to function as the initial clearing house for those pupils unfitted to take up the higher class work. The successful sixth graders pass on to undergo another and at the same time more severe selective strain in the seventh grade. Those that survive this final ordeal enter the comparatively easy final grade. Only 3.1 per cent of the present pupils of the eighth grade failed therein.

TABLE 46b

SAME IN PER CENTS

Using Total of Promoted and Non-Promoted as the Base

Grades	Eighth	Seventh	Sixth	Fifth	Fourth	Third	Second	First
	per cent	per cent	per cent	per cent	per cent	per cent	per cent	per cent
Eighth	3.1	20.0	10.8	10.0	5.4	6.2	7.7	30.8
Seventh		14.0	18.4	7.2	6.8	5.3	6.3	30.0
Sixth			16.1	10.4	8.7	6.5	7.0	32.2
Fifth				15.2	13.3	6.3	5.7	39.2
Aver.	3.1	16.3	15.7	10.5	8.6	6.1	6.6	32.8

In Table 46 b, on comparing the pupils now in the eighth, seventh, sixth, and fifth grades who repeated the third grade, little variation is apparent.

	THIRD GRADE per cent
In eighth grade	6.2
In seventh grade	5.3
In sixth grade	6.5
In fifth grade	6.3
Median	6.25

The chances of any of the pupils of the grammar grades having been left back in the third grade are about the same. The ratio is 1 to 16.

The same holds true on comparing those in the eighth and seventh with those in the sixth and fifth taken together respectively. In the fourth grade, however, the fifth and sixth grade pupils have on the average failed twice as frequently as the seventh and eighth grade pupils.

The special treatment of retardation in this and the preceding chapters being limited to the study of the so-called initial starters, it is unfortunate that in the city of Plainfield where the full history cards are recorded that only 485 cases were obtainable. One notes in some of the tables showing the age-grade relations, promotion and non-promotion statistics, and the accompanying sex distributions, violations of certain tendencies gleaned from the tables of the previous systems. It may be that Plainfield is rather different from the other cities, or on the other hand, the number of cases being somewhat meagre may possibly account for the odd distributions. However, in Table 46 b the general tendency relative to the difficulty of the various grades indicates the same scale of increase from the second through the seventh grade.

CHAPTER VII

SUMMARY

GRAMMAR GRADE PUPILS. 3,865 CASES

The records of the initial starters in the school systems tabulated in the foregoing chapters indicate definite tendencies. The summary is confined to the cases in the grammar grades only. Table 47 indicates in number the sex distribution of the pupils in the five cities visited.

TABLE 47

ACTUAL NUMBER OF CASES INVESTIGATED

Personal Study of 3,865 Initial Starters in the Grammar Grades of Schools Selected at Random in FIVE Cities

Cities	Schools	Boys	Girls	Total
East Orange, N. J.	4	162	165	327
Plainfield, N. J.	4	258	227	485
Elizabeth, N. J.	5	422	447	869
New York City, N. Y. (One school district.)	6	474	464	938
Paterson, N. J.	5	617	629	1,246
Total	24	1,933	1,932	3,865

Eliminating the fourth grade cases, the most number of records were obtained from Paterson, the least from East Orange. By mere chance the boys and girls were found almost evenly distributed. Of the total 3,865 initial starters in the twenty-four schools, 1,933 were boys and 1,932, girls.

THE MIGRATION OF PUPILS

The per cents of initial starters in the grammar grades based on the current register at the time of visitation are shown in Table 48 and in graphic illustration, Chart 19.

TABLE 48

PER CENTS OF INITIAL STARTERS IN GRAMMAR GRADES

Grades	8B	8A	7B	7A	6B	6A	5B	5A	Aver. of Gross Per Cents
Cities									
New York	43.7	37.0	38.5	32.0	44.7	41.2	45.5	52.0	41.9
	40.4		35.3		43.0		48.8		
Paterson[1]	48.3	51.0	47.4	55.4	50.3	40.1	49.1	50.3	49.0
	49.7		51.4		45.2		49.7		
Elizabeth	32.9		33.6		37.0		51.5		38.8
Plainfield	56.0		53.0		57.0		56.0		55.5
East Orange	39.9		33.8		30.4		43.3		36.9
Medians	40.4		35.3		43.0		49.7		41.9

[1]The order of grades in Paterson is: 8A, 8B, 7A, 7B, 6A, 6B, 5A, 5B.

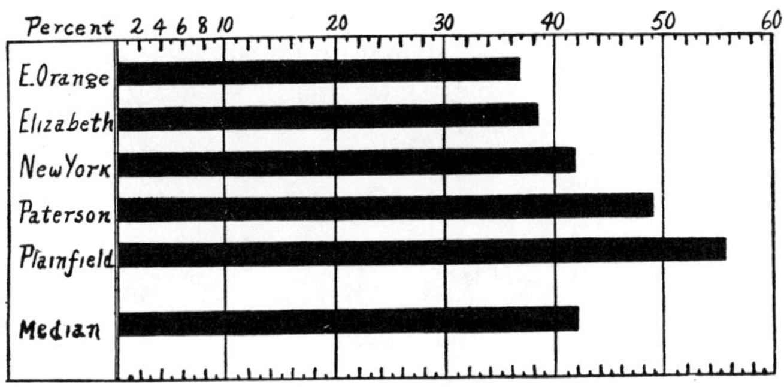

CHART 19. Approximate percentages of initial starters in grammar grades

The median per cents in the five cities show that 40.4 per cent of the registered eighth grade pupils entered the schools in which they now attend; 35.3 per cent in the case of the seventh grade; 43.0 per cent in the sixth grade; and 49.7 per cent in the fifth grade. The median of the averages of gross per cents in all the grammar grades is 41.9 per cent. That is, more than half of the present grammar grade pupils either migrated to the schools in which they now attend, from other schools in the community or elsewhere, and were admitted by transfer, or they entered their present schools in some grade later than the first as new admissions.

Obviously, to take the average percentage instead of the median would be incorrect in view of the situation in Plainfield. (See Chapter VI, page 81.) Note that the New York schools register the tendency in the eighth, seventh, and sixth grades.

One may safely say that less than 50 per cent of the grammar grade children of these city school systems have been under the entire charge of their present schools from the first grade up. In Chart 19 the relative comparison of systems in this respect is plainly evident. Paterson, in which city retardation is less frequent as compared with any of the other cities, has at the same time a larger percentage of initial starters in its grammar department. The city of Plainfield, for reasons previously stated, is not considered.

Age-Grade Relations

Concerning the 3,865 grammar grade initial starters, Table 49 shows in hundredths the retardation by grades.

TABLE 49

Retardation in Per Cents in Grammar Grades

<table>
<tr><th>Grades</th><th>8B</th><th>8A</th><th>7B</th><th>7A</th><th>6B</th><th>6A</th><th>5B</th><th>5A</th></tr>
<tr><td>Cities</td><td colspan="8"></td></tr>
<tr><td rowspan="2">New York</td><td>66.3</td><td>76.9</td><td>84.4</td><td>75.8</td><td>85.5</td><td>67.6</td><td>84.8</td><td>71.7</td></tr>
<tr><td colspan="2">70.9</td><td colspan="2">80.1</td><td colspan="2">76.3</td><td colspan="2">78.5</td></tr>
<tr><td rowspan="2">Paterson</td><td>48.1</td><td>33.3</td><td>51.2</td><td>39.8</td><td>58.0</td><td>44.3</td><td>63.3</td><td>35.9</td></tr>
<tr><td colspan="2">40.2</td><td colspan="2">45.1</td><td colspan="2">51.9</td><td colspan="2">48.4</td></tr>
<tr><td>Elizabeth</td><td colspan="2">61.5</td><td colspan="2">72.7</td><td colspan="2">78.0</td><td colspan="2">84.5</td></tr>
<tr><td>Plainfield</td><td colspan="2">78.8</td><td colspan="2">67.2</td><td colspan="2">75.2</td><td colspan="2">73.0</td></tr>
<tr><td>East Orange</td><td colspan="2">77.1</td><td colspan="2">79.3</td><td colspan="2">78.9</td><td colspan="2">83.5</td></tr>
<tr><td>Medians</td><td colspan="2">70.9</td><td colspan="2">72.7</td><td colspan="2">76.3</td><td colspan="2">78.5</td></tr>
</table>

Percent 10 20 30 40 50 60 70 80 100 | 10 20 30 40 50 60 70 80 | 10 20 30 40 50 60 70 80 | 10 20 30 40 50 60 70 80
Grades | Fifth | Sixth | Seventh | Eighth
E. Orange
Elizabeth
New York
Paterson
Plainfield

CHART 20. Percentages of retardation in grammar grades; assuming 10 years to 10 years 11 months inclusive as the normal entrance age to the fifth grade

To permit of comparison with the other cities, in New York City and Paterson the half-yearly grades are averaged in the following manner: For example, from Chapter II, page 22, one learns that 55, 8 B pupils and 50, 8 A pupils are above normal age. The total numbers of cases in these grades are 83 and 65 respectively. The sum $50 + 55 = 105$ is divided by the sum $83 + 65 = 148$ to obtain 70.9 per cent, the average percentage of retardation in the eighth grade.

The median percentages of retardation in the grammar grades, assuming 10 years to 10 years 11 months inclusive as the normal entrance age to the fifth grade, are all above 70 per cent. In the eighth, sixth, and fifth grades New York City again indicates the tendency. In Paterson the deviations from the medians are by far the greatest.

Allowing one year on the assumed theoretical age-limit, these percentages reduce considerably. The medians now become: Eighth grade, 36.9; seventh grade, 39.1; sixth grade, 40.8; fifth grade, 45.1. That is, 36.9 per cent of the present eighth grade pupils were more than 14 years 11 months when they entered the eighth grade; 39.1 per cent were more than 13 years 11 months when they entered the seventh grade; 40.8 per cent were more than 12 years 11 months when they entered the sixth grade; and 45.1 per cent were more than 11 years 11 months when they entered the fifth grade. The progressive decrease from the fifth grade to the eighth grade inclusive indicates clearly the effect of increasing elimination.

Comparing the grammar grade girls and boys in the matter of retardation, Table 50 and the accompanying charts show the age-grade relations by city and grades.

TABLE 50

RETARDATION IN PER CENTS IN GRAMMAR GRADES. SEX DISTRIBUTION

Boys in plain type. Girls in italics.

Grades	8B	8A	7B	7A	6B	6A	5B	5A
Cities								
New York	*67.5* 65.1	*75.0* 78.0	*80.9* 87.8	*75.0* 76.7	*84.6* 86.3	*72.9* 62.7	*89.9* 80.0	*63.2* 83.1
	70.3 71.4		*77.8* 82.6		*78.5* 74.3		*75.9* 81.3	
Paterson	*51.4* 44.1	*24.6* 40.2	*50.5* 52.3	*39.1* 40.4	*56.2* 59.8	*32.8* 54.8	*64.9* 61.3	*29.9* 41.1
	38.5 41.8		*45.1* 45.1		*46.2* 57.5		*47.4* 49.3	
Elizabeth	*57.8* 65.2		*66.7* 78.4		*76.5* 79.6		*79.9* 89.7	
Plainfield	*76.6* 81.6		*61.7* 72.1		*81.7* 69.8		*67.3* 77.3	
East Orange	*77.4* 76.9		*77.3* 83.3		*79.3* 78.6		*76.9* 88.5	
Medians	*70.3* 71.4		*66.7* 78.4		*78.5* 74.3		*75.9* 81.3	

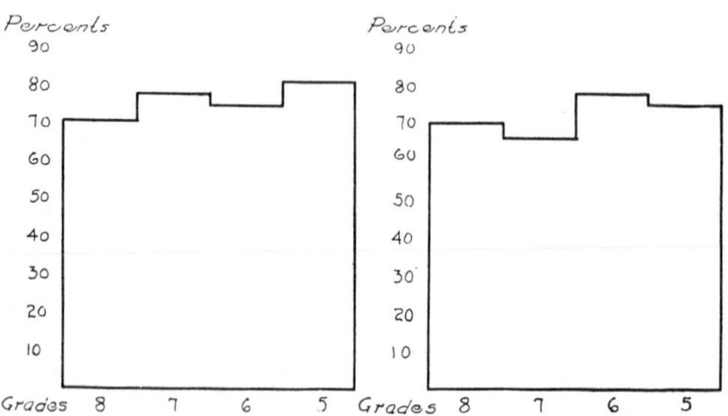

CHART 21 a. Median percentages of retarded boys

CHART 21 b. Median percentages of retarded girls

Reading from Table 50 it appears that the boys are retarded more often than the girls. The median percentage of retarded girls in the sixth grade, 78.5 per cent, is larger than that recorded in the case of the boys. In two out of the five cities, however, there are larger proportions of "over-age" boys in this grade also. The medians in the sex classification table are the same in hundredths as those of New York City, excepting for grade seven, wherein Elizabeth registers the middle tendency.

The summary table showing the distribution of "over-ageness" at the time of entrance to the first grade follows. Six years to 6 years 11 months is the assumed normal entrance age in Table 51 and Charts 22 and 23.

TABLE 51

"Over-Ageness" in Per Cents at Time of Entrance to First Grade

Grades	8B	8A	7B	7A	6B	6A	5B	5A	Average
Cities New York	48.2	46.2	59.4	53.7	46.4	40.7	47.6	57.9	49.8
	47.3		56.5		43.5		52.5		
Paterson	24.0	18.4	19.8	30.6	23.9	18.6	27.3	19.8	23.0
	21.0		25.6		21.5		23.2		
Elizabeth	56.2		55.8		68.3		74.5		66.5
Plainfield	29.4		23.4		32.5		42.6		32.0
East Orange	38.1		37.8		40.3		50.5		41.9
Medians	38.1		37.8		40.3		50.5		41.9

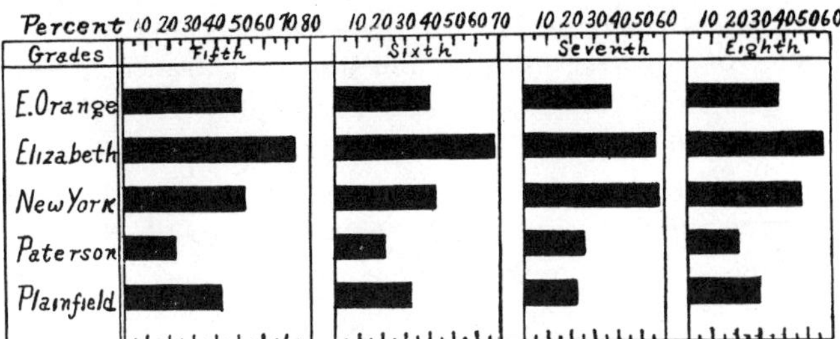

Chart 22. Percentages of "over-ageness" at time of entrance to the first grade: assuming 6 years to 6 years 11 months inclusive as the normal entrance age

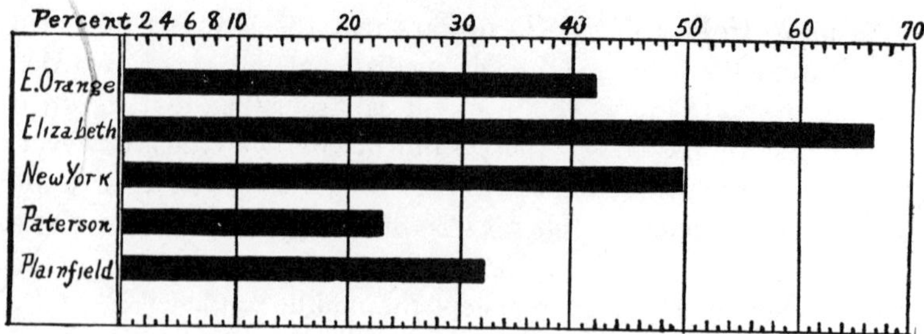

CHART 23. Average percentages of "over-ageness" at time of entrance to first grade

The East Orange system indicates the median tendency in the matter of initial "over-ageness." Of the eighth grade pupils 38.1 per cent were above 6 years 11 months at school entrance; seventh grade, 37.8 per cent; sixth grade, 40.3 per cent; fifth grade, 50.5 per cent. Taking the median of the averages of all grades,[1] one finds that 41.9 per cent of the children now in the grammar grades were "over-age" at the time of entrance to the first grade. Whereas in each of the grammar grades over 70 per cent are at present retarded (see Table 49), the percentage of pupils who were above the normal age assumed, when they were admitted to the first grade, is approximately 40 per cent.

The "over-age" pupils based on the initial age records of the 1,933 boys and the 1,932 girls are distributed in the next table. The median percentages of "over-age" boys and girls may be compared in the appended graphic illustrations.

Although the median of the averages for the five cities would indicate that more boys as compared with girls were above 6 years 11 months when they began school, in grades seven and six the reverse is the tendency. That boys are more variable in the matter of "over-ageness" at the time of entrance to the first grade is apparent in Charts 24 a and 24 b. It is necessary, however, to constantly keep in mind the fact that all the conclusions in this summary refer to that select class of children who entered the first grade, have remained through the primary grades, and are now in the grammar department of the school in which they were originally admitted.

[1] These averages are reckoned as follows: e.g., In the case of New York City the quotient obtained by dividing the sum of the numbers of the initial "over-age" pupils in all the grammar grades by the sum of the total number of cases studied is changed to per cent.

TABLE 52

"OVER-AGENESS" IN PER CENTS AT TIME OF ENTRANCE TO FIRST GRADE. SEX DISTRIBUTION

Boys in plain type. Girls in italics.

Grades	8B	8A	7B	7A	6B	6A	5B	5A	Average
Cities									
New York	*40.0* 55.8	*45.8* 46.3	*59.6* 59.2	*44.2* 65.1	*41.5* 50.7	*40.0* 41.3	*45.6* 49.4	*55.2* 61.5	*46.8* 52.7
	42.2 51.2		*51.5* 62.0		*40.7* 45.7		*50.6* 54.7		
Paterson	*21.4* 27.1	*18.5* 18.3	*21.6* 16.9	*28.7* 32.3	*29.2* 18.4	*20.9* 16.4	*26.0* 29.0	*19.5* 20.0	*23.5* 22.4
	20.0 22.0		*25.0* 26.2		*25.6* 17.5		*22.7* 23.7		
Elizabeth	*37.5* 74.2		*52.4* 59.1		*64.3* 72.8.		*67.4* 82.5		*59.5* 73.9
Plainfield	*31.9* 26.3		*21.7* 25.0		*32.4* 32.6		*53.1* 34.8		*33.9* 30.2
East Orange	*35.8* 40.4		*38.6* 36.7		*48.3* 32.1		*43.6* 55.8		*40.6* 43.2
Medians	*35.8* 40.4		*38.6* 36.7		*40.7* 32.6		*50.6* 54.7		*40.6* 43.2

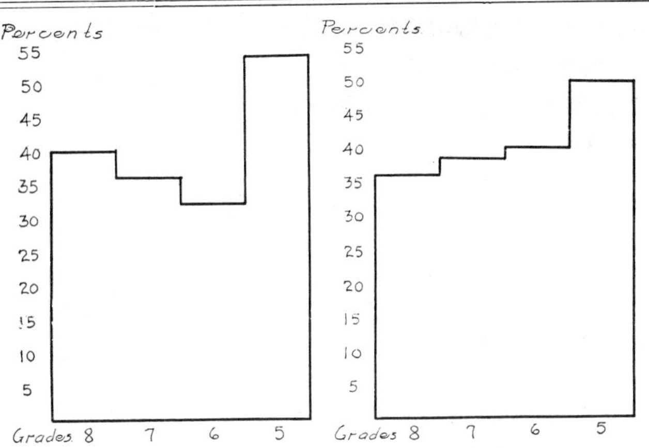

CHART 24 a. Boys CHART 24 b. Girls
Median percentages of initial "over-ageness"

THE INCIDENCE OF RETARDATION

The relative frequency of regularly promoted and non-promoted eighth grade pupils is summarized in Table 53. The accompanying charts illustrate the median percentages of regularly promoted pupils and of those left back one, two, three, four, and five times.

TABLE 53

PERCENTAGES OF EIGHTH GRADE PUPILS REPEATING AND NON-REPEATING DURING SCHOOL LIFE

Cities	None		One		Two		Three		Four		Five	
	8B	8A	8B	8A	8B	8A	8B	8A	8B	8A	8B	8A
New York	43	26	24	35	25	26	2	11	4	2	1	0
	36		29		26		6		3		1	
Paterson	47	44	28	31	23	17	2	6	0	1	0	0
	45		30		20		4		1		0	
Elizabeth	71		22		5		1		1		0	
Plainfield	9		48		32		10		0		0	
East Orange	63		29		9		0		0		0	
Medians	45		29		20		4		1		0	

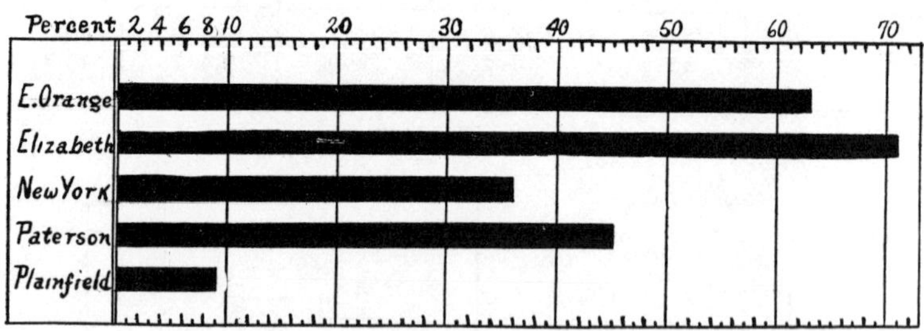

CHART 25. Percentages of eighth grade pupils never left back during entire school life

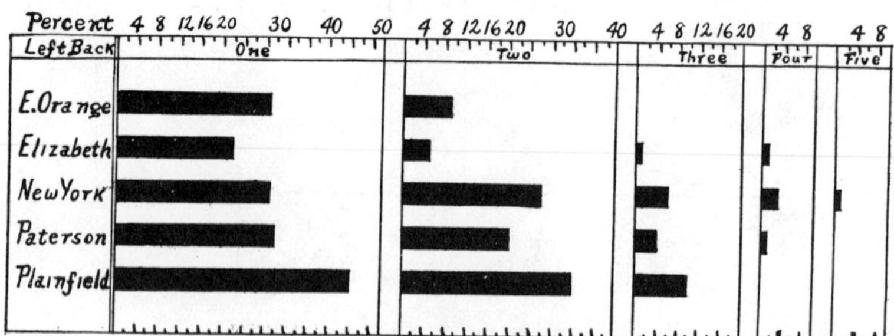

CHART 26. Percentages of eighth grade pupils repeating during entire school life

Of the eighth grade pupils who entered the first grade of the school in which they now attend, 45 per cent as a median have never been left back during their entire school life; 29 per cent have repeated once; 20 per cent, twice; 4 per cent, three times; and 1 per cent, four times. It is justifiable to say that of those selected pupils who reach the highest grade, the tendency is to be left back once during their school life. In Elizabeth and East Orange the mode falls in the "no-time" group. Eliminating Plainfield, these cities deviate most from the median percentage of regularly promoted children.

Distributing the eighth grade pupils according to sex, Table 54 shows the relative frequencies as percentages of eighth grade boys and girls promoted and non-promoted throughout the grades. The median percentages are stated in the bottom row.

TABLE 54

EIGHTH GRADE PUPILS REPEATING AND NON-REPEATING DURING SCHOOL LIFE. SEX DISTRIBUTION IN PER CENTS

Boys in plain type. Girls in italics.

<table>
<tr><th rowspan="2">Cities</th><th colspan="2">None</th><th colspan="2">One</th><th colspan="2">Two</th><th colspan="2">Three</th><th colspan="2">Four</th><th colspan="2">Five</th></tr>
<tr><th>8B</th><th>8A</th><th>8B</th><th>8A</th><th>8B</th><th>8A</th><th>8B</th><th>8A</th><th>8B</th><th>8A</th><th>8B</th><th>8A</th></tr>
<tr><td rowspan="2">New York</td><td>37.5
48.8</td><td>29.2
24.4</td><td>30.0
18.6</td><td>50.0
26.8</td><td>27.5
23.3</td><td>16.7
31.7</td><td>2.5
2.3</td><td>4.2
14.6</td><td>2.5
4.7</td><td>0.0
2.4</td><td>0.0
2.3</td><td>0.0
0.0</td></tr>
<tr><td colspan="2">34.4
36.9</td><td colspan="2">37.5
22.6</td><td colspan="2">23.4
27.4</td><td colspan="2">3.1
8.3</td><td colspan="2">1.6
3.6</td><td colspan="2">0.0
1.2</td></tr>
<tr><td rowspan="2">Paterson</td><td>52.9
39.0</td><td>46.2
42.7</td><td>31.4
23.7</td><td>33.8
29.3</td><td>15.7
32.2</td><td>18.5
15.9</td><td>0.0
5.1</td><td>1.5
9.8</td><td>0.0
0.0</td><td>0.0
2.4</td><td>0.0
0.0</td><td>0.0
0.0</td></tr>
<tr><td colspan="2">49.6
41.1</td><td colspan="2">32.6
27.0</td><td colspan="2">17.0
22.7</td><td colspan="2">0.7
7.8</td><td colspan="2">0.0
1.4</td><td colspan="2">0.0
0.0</td></tr>
<tr><td>Elizabeth</td><td colspan="2">73.4
68.2</td><td colspan="2">21.9
22.7</td><td colspan="2">3.1
7.6</td><td colspan="2">0.0
1.5</td><td colspan="2">1.6
0.0</td><td colspan="2">0.0
0.0</td></tr>
<tr><td>Plainfield</td><td colspan="2">10.6
7.9</td><td colspan="2">44.7
52.6</td><td colspan="2">31.9
31.6</td><td colspan="2">12.8
7.9</td><td colspan="2">0.0
0.0</td><td colspan="2">0.0
0.0</td></tr>
<tr><td>East Orange</td><td colspan="2">58.5
67.3</td><td colspan="2">34.0
23.1</td><td colspan="2">7.5
9.6</td><td colspan="2">0.0
0.0</td><td colspan="2">0.0
0.0</td><td colspan="2">0.0
0.0</td></tr>
<tr><td>Medians</td><td colspan="2">49.6
41.4</td><td colspan="2">34.0
22.7</td><td colspan="2">17.0
22.7</td><td colspan="2">0.7
7.8</td><td colspan="2">0.0
0.0</td><td colspan="2">0.0
0.0</td></tr>
</table>

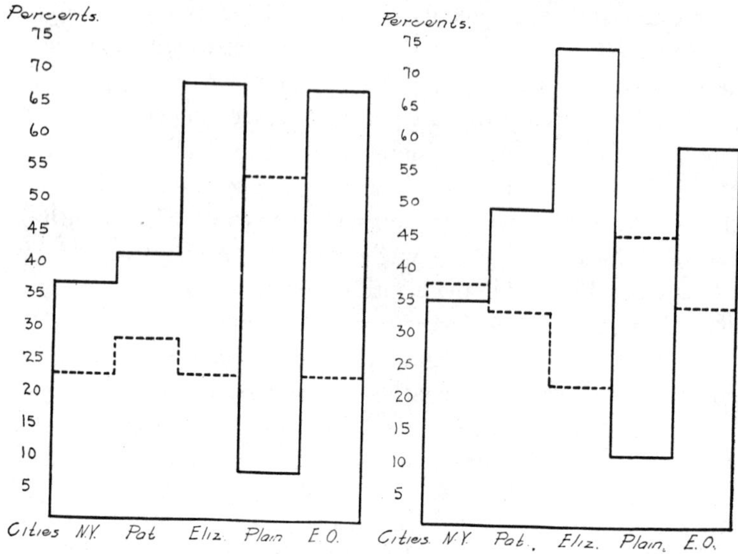

CHART 27 a. —— Eighth grade boys never left back during entire school life. ---- Eighth grade boys left back once

CHART 27 b. —— Eighth grade girls never left back during entire school life. ---- Eighth grade girls left back once

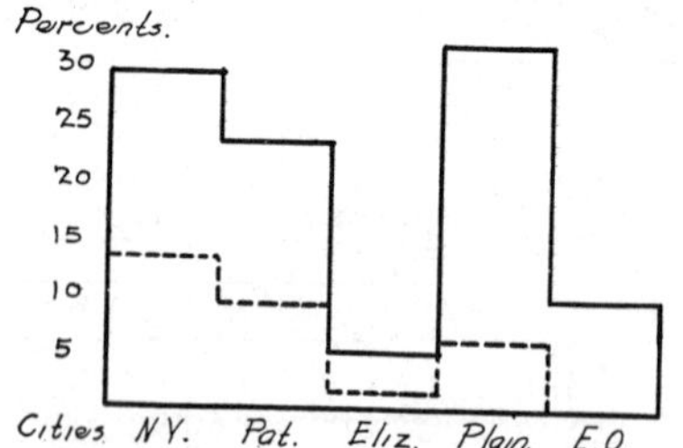

CHART 28 a. Eighth grade boys left back two and three or more times during school life
—— Two times. ---- Three or more times

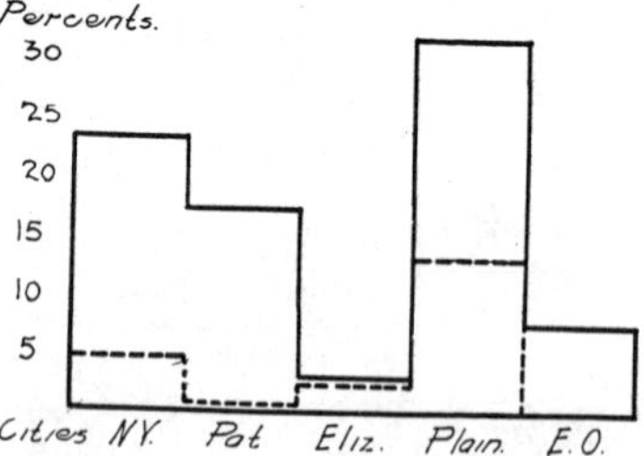

CHART 28 b. Eighth grade girls left back two and three or more times during school life
—— Two times. ---- Three or more times

In the case of regular promotion and "one-time" repetition the girls record larger percentages, whereas the boys are more frequently left back two and three times. In New York City and East Orange the girls maintain the average position in the distribution curve of mental ability, such ability being measured solely on the basis of relative frequency in the grades. The boys on the other hand in these cities occupy the extremes of the distribution. Larger percentages of them have advanced regularly and at the same time more of them have repeated two, three, and more times. In Paterson and Elizabeth the girls unquestionably are brighter than the boys. In the former city the mode in the case of the eighth grade girls is in the "no-time" group while the selected boys tend to be left back once during school life. In Plainfield the boys who finally reach the eighth grade must be credited with the better records. From the medians as read in the bottom row of Table 54, one notes the larger range in relative ability on the part of the boys. The Paterson system records the median tendency of the five cities.

The fact that the girls who reach the eighth grade in general have been more successful throughout the entire school course in the matter of regular promotion and relative frequency of repetition does not of necessity reflect discredit on the boys. It may sanction the charge that the modern course of study is not sufficiently adapted to the special needs and inherent capacities of the latter.

The grade distributions of non-promotion as percentages of the total number promoted and non-promoted in the various school systems are shown in Tables 55, 56, 57, 58, and Charts 29 through 32.

Reading from Table 55, the bottom row of percentages record with considerable accuracy the prevailing tendencies in the five city school systems. Four and four tenths per cent of the eighth grade pupils who remain through all the grades of the school they originally entered are left back in the eighth grade; 9.5 per cent, in the seventh grade; 7 per cent, in the sixth; 4.6 per cent, in the fifth; 4.3 per cent, in the fourth; 3.9 per cent, in the third; 2.4 per cent, in the second; and 3.5 per cent, in the first. It is evident that the seventh grade marks the chief obstacle in the progress of the pupil who persists in school. The increasing difficulty of the grades from the first till the eighth is clearly manifest. This holds true of the two systems with half-yearly terms as well as in the case of those cities having the yearly series of grades. In New York City the 6 B and 7 A grades show the highest percentages of retention. In Paterson evidently the upper seventh is the most difficult.

TABLE 55

Grade Distribution Indicating Relative Frequency of Non-Promotion in Hundredths

Eighth Grade Pupils Only

Grades	8B	8A	7B	7A	6B	6A	5B	5A	4B	4A	3B	3A	2B	2A	1B	1A
Cities New York	5.8	5.0	7.7	11.3	11.3	5.0	5.9	5.0	4.1	4.1	3.6	4.1	0.9	2.3	0.9	1.4
	5.3		9.5		8.2		5.5		4.1		3.9		1.6		2.3	
Paterson	3.6	4.2	9.1	6.6	4.2	5.8	3.6	5.5	5.0	3.6	2.2	3.9	1.7	3.0	2.8	2.5
	4.0		7.9		5.0		4.6		4.3		3.0		2.4		2.6	
Elizabeth	5.6		9.2		2.1		2.1		4.2		4.9		3.5		3.5	
Plainfield	3.1		20.0		10.8		10.0		5.4		6.2		7.7		30.8	
East Orange	4.4		14.9		7.0		4.4		4.4		2.6		0.9		3.5	
Medians	4.4		9.5		7.0		4.6		4.3		3.9		2.4		3.5	

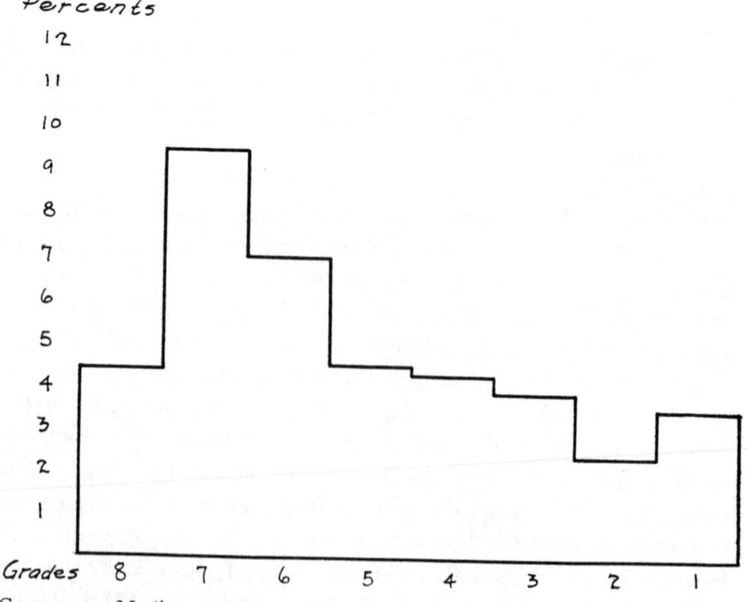

Chart 29. Median percentages of eighth grade pupils showing the incidence of retardation

TABLE 56

GRADE DISTRIBUTION INDICATING RELATIVE FREQUENCY OF NON-PROMOTION IN HUNDREDTHS

Seventh Grade Pupils Only

Grades	7B	7A	6B	6A	5B	5A	4B	4A	3B	3A	2B	2A	1B	1A
Cities New York	13.8	11.5	7.1	9.2	6.1	8.5	5.4	6.1	3.7	4.1	1.4	2.7	1.7	2.7
	12.2		8.1		7.3		5.8		3.9		2.0		2.2	
Paterson	8.1	8.0	5.6	4.9	6.5	6.0	5.4	4.2	4.2	3.6	3.1	2.7	3.3	2.2
	8.1		5.3		6.3		4.8		3.9		2.9		2.8	
Elizabeth	12.4		4.7		4.1		2.6		4.1		5.7		7.8	
Plainfield	14.0		18.4		7.2		6.8		5.3		6.3		30.0	
East Orange.	11.4		7.6		8.9		6.3		2.5		3.8		5.1	
Medians	12.2		7.6		7.2		5.8		3.9		3.8		5.1	

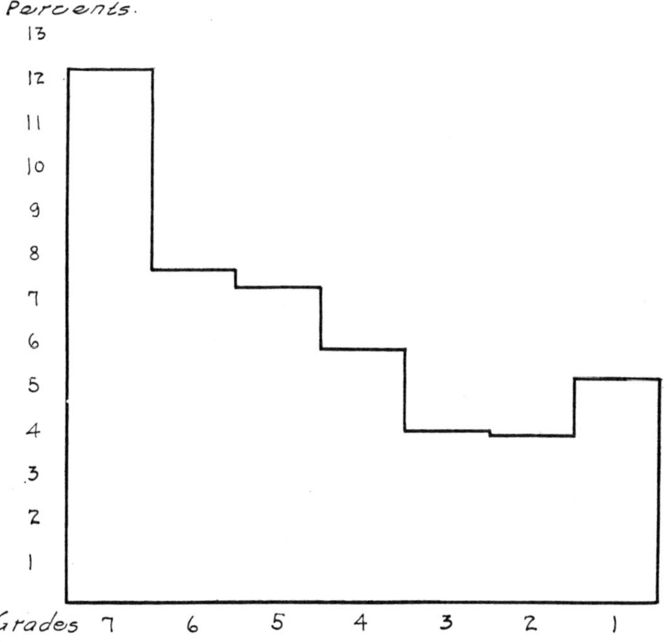

CHART 30. Median percentages of seventh grade pupils showing the incidence of retardation

TABLE 57

GRADE DISTRIBUTION INDICATING RELATIVE FREQUENCY OF NON-PROMOTION IN HUNDREDTHS

Sixth Grade Pupils Only

Grades	6B	6A	5B	5A	4B	4A	3B	3A	2B	2A	1B	1A
Cities												
New York	10.6	10.1	11.2	9.9	7.4	7.9	8.3	6.1	4.8	5.0	2.0	3.3
	10.2		10.5		7.7		7.2		4.9		2.6	
Paterson	10.2	10.3	7.0	6.0	5.5	4.1	6.7	5.8	2.6	3.8	3.4	3.6
	10.3		6.5		4.8		6.2		3.2		3.5	
Elizabeth	12.3		10.2		9.8		5.3		3.7		4.1	
Plainfield	16.1		10.4		8.7		6.5		7.0		32.2	
East Orange	13.8		7.7		4.6		6.2		6.2		7.7	
Medians	12.3		10.2		7.7		6.2		4.9		4.1	

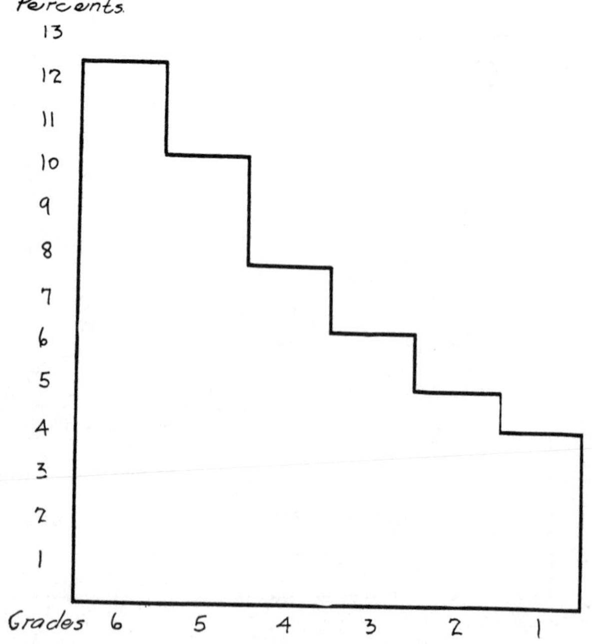

CHART 31. Median percentage of sixth grade pupils showing the incidence of retardation

TABLE 58

GRADE DISTRIBUTION INDICATING RELATIVE FREQUENCY OF NON-PROMOTION IN HUNDREDTHS

Fifth Grade Pupils Only

Grades	5B	5A	4B	4A	3B	3A	2B	2A	1B	1A
Cities New York	12.4	10.5	8.5	9.9	9.1	10.1	8.0	5.2	3.7	6.4
	11.2		9.2		9.6		6.6		5.0	
Paterson	5.9	10.9	7.4	4.4	7.4	5.7	6.4	4.0	4.7	5.0
	9.4		5.9		6.5		5.2		4.8	
Elizabeth	19.0		12.1		10.1		8.1		7.2	
Plainfield	15.2		13.3		6.3		5.7		39.2	
East Orange	10.2		7.2		7.2		10.2		8.2	
Medians	11.2		9.2		7.2		6.6		7.2	

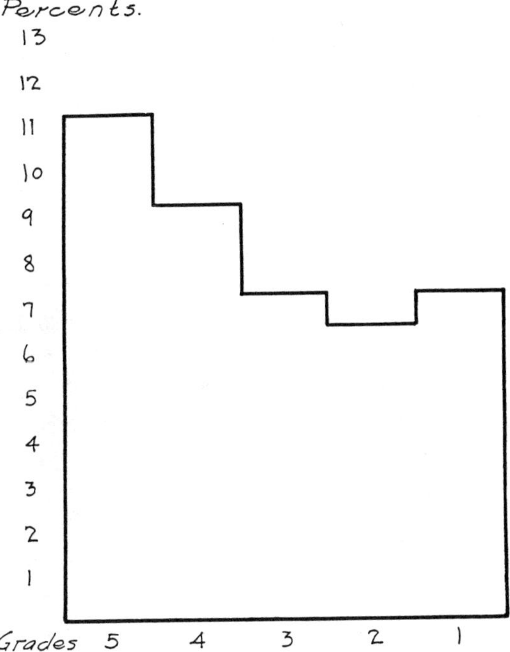

CHART 32. Median percentages of fifth grade pupils showing the incidence of retardation

That the pupils find the lower much easier than the upper grades is the definite tendency as shown in the foregoing tables. Table 55 indicates the seventh grade with a median of 9.5 per cent as having been the most difficult grade for the present eighth grade pupils. Table 56 indicates the seventh grade again with a median of 12.2 per cent as the most difficult grade for the present seventh grade pupils. In Table 57 the sixth grade pupils show the largest percentages of non-promotion in their present grade. The progress of the fifth grade pupils according to Table 58 is impeded more in the fifth grade than in any of the preceding grades. In grades five, six, and especially seven, the chances of retardation in the case of any given pupil are decidedly more than in any of the other grades. The pupil who is fortunate enough to withstand the strain of the difficult seventh grade is practically offered the assurance of success on entrance to the comparatively easy graduating class.

Taken generally the grammar grades exert much more pressure on the pupils in the matter of retardation. It is more than probable that, were all the "hold-overs" in grades one through four to remain in school, the percentages of retardation in the upper grades would be still larger.

Tables 55 to 58 record the distribution of non-promotion in hundredths of the grammar grade initial starters. These pupils represent a selected class as compared with the children migrating from school to school. It is fair to suppose that, were the histories of these shifting pupils studied, the same progressive increase in grade frequency would be the characteristic tendency.

The records of the initial starters were obtained from the individual pupils in class room and were checked by a careful study of the individual history cards. These cards registered accurately the frequency of grammar grade retention. In the case of non-promotion in the primary grades, where the official records were not obtainable, errors of memory would necessitate some correction of the recorded percentages. Even with a generous corrective allowance there is every reason to believe that the classes would still be progressively harder from the first to the last year of the school. At any rate the burden of proof rests upon those who fancy that a pupil is more likely to suffer retardation in early than in late grades.

BIBLIOGRAPHY

Books

AYRES, L. P.* Laggards in Our Schools; a Study of Retardation and Elimination in City Systems. New York: Russell Sage Foundation Publications, 1909.

BONSER, F. G. The Reasoning Ability of Children of the Fourth, Fifth, and Sixth School Grades. New York: Teachers College, Columbia University, 1910.

CORNMAN, O. P.* Promotion and Retardation in the Elementary Schools. Philadelphia: 1906.

DUTTON, S. T. and SNEDDEN, D. S.* Administration of Public Education in the United States. New York: Macmillan Company, 1908.

GULICK, L. H. and AYRES, L. P.* Medical Inspection of Schools. New York: Russell Sage Foundation Publications, 1908.

MAENNEL, B. Auxiliary Education; The Training of Backward Children. Trans. by EMMA SYLVESTER. New York: Doubleday, Page & Co. 1909.

SNEDDEN, D. S. and ALLEN, W. H.* School Reports and School Efficiency. New York: Macmillan Company, 1908.

THORNDIKE, E. L.* Educational Psychology. New York: Teachers College, Columbia University, 1910.

———.* Theory of Mental and Social Measurements. New York, Science Press, 1904.

The following reports were examined in order to check the statistical conclusions of some of the investigations referred to in this study.

General Reports

REPORT OF THE COMMISSIONER OF EDUCATION. Vol. 2, 1907:577. Statistics of City School Systems.

———. Vol. 2, 1908:1057. Summary of Statistical Tables.

———. Vol. 2, 1909:1343. Retardation and Acceleration of Pupils in City Schools.

DEPARTMENT OF INTERIOR. Bureau of Education. Bulletin No. 4, 1907. The Elimination of Pupils from School. E. L. THORNDIKE.

———. Bureau of Education. Bulletin No. 5, 1911. G. D. STRAYER.

REPORT OF COMMISSIONER OF EDUCATION OF NEW YORK STATE. 1908: 610; 1910:32.

REPORT OF COMMITTEE ON DELINQUENT AND DEPENDENT CHILDREN. State Association of Town and City Superintendents. 1908:3–25.

* Special reference is made to this study.

City Reports

Baltimore, Md. Annual Report of Board of School Commissioners. 1908:51, 119.

Boston, Mass. Report of School Committee. June, 1909:20; July, 1909:22.

Brooklyn, N. Y. Tenth Annual Report of New York City Superintendent. 1908:68.

Chicago, Ill. Report of Board of Education. 1899:123.

Cincinnati, O. Annual Report of the Public Schools. 1909:55.

Columbus, O. Report of Public Schools. 1902:200.

East Orange, N. J. Annual School Report. 1905:19; 1907:56.

Kansas City, Mo. Annual Report of Board of Education. 1907:88.

Louisville, Ky. Report of School Board. 1907:127.

Medford, Mass. Annual Report of School Committee. 1907:17. 1908:17.

New Haven, Conn. Report of Board of Education. 1908:28.

New York City, N. Y. Sixth Annual Report of City Superintendent of Schools. 1904:42-49. Twelfth Annual Report. 1910:225.

Paterson, N. J. Annual Report of Public Schools. 1908:159; 1909:110.

Philadelphia, Pa. Report of Board of Public Education. 1907:24 (Statements J and K); 1908:92 (Tables 16–37).

Plainfield, N. J. Report of Board of Education. 1908:47; 1909:37

Reading, Pa. Biennial Report of Board of Education. 1907:95.

Rochester, N. Y. Annual Report of the Public Schools. 1897:7, 30.

San Francisco, Cal. Annual Report of the Public Schools. 1892:7.

Springfield, O. Annual Report of Public Schools. 1908:31, 53.

Trenton, N. J. Annual Report of Commissioners of Public Instruction. 1897:204.

Wheeling, W. Va. Annual Report of Public Schools. 1907:19.

Articles from Periodicals

Educational Review.* 1909:122. Retardation, its Significance and its Requirements. R. P. Falkner.

———.* 1909:342. Retardation of Pupils in their Studies. J. M. Greenwood.

———.* 1910:48. Elimination and Repetition. F. P. Bachman.

———. 1910:121. A Neglected Cause of Retardation. W. D. Sheldon.

Elementary School Teacher. 1910:326. England and her Retarded Children. H. Leather.

———.* 1910:409. Repeaters in the Upper Grammar Grades. E. L. Thorndike.

Journal of Educational Psychology. 1910:61.* Individual Differences in Grammar Grade Children. W. G. Chambers.

———. 1910:132. The Subnormal Child in New York City Schools. M. S. Macy.

———. 1910:435. The Binet Scale for Measuring Intelligence and Retardation. E. B. Huey.

———. 1911:3. Measuring Results in Education. G. D. Strayer.

*Special reference is made to this study.

*N. E. A. Proceedings.** 1902:215. The Danger of Using Biological Analogies in Reasoning on Educational Subjects. W. T. HARRIS.

———. 1908:155. Democracy and Education; Equal Opportunity for All. J. E. RUSSELL. Discussion: 159. E. C. ELLIOTT.

———. 1908:348. Provision for Exceptional Children. J. H. VAN SICKLE.

———. 1910:980. The Standardization of School Statistics. H. R. M. COOK.

*Psychological Clinic.** Vol. I, No. 2. April 1907:41. A Method for Determining the Extent and Causes of Retardation in a City School System. J. E. BRYAN.

———. Vol. I, No. 4. June, 1907:97. Clinical Studies of Retarded Children. G. W. TWITMEYER.

———.* Vol. I, No. 8. Jan. 1908:245. The Retardation of the Pupils of Five City School Systems. O. P. CORNMAN.

———.* Vol. II, No. 3. May 1908:57. Some Further Considerations upon the Retardation of the Pupils of Five City School Systems. R. P. FALKNER.

———. Vol. II, No. 8. Jan. 1909:227. Some Uses of Statistics in the Supervision of Schools. R. P. FALKNER.

———. Vol. III, No. 2. April 1909:29. Orthogenics in the Public Schools. L. WITMER.

———. Vol. III, No. 6. Nov. 1909:164. Retardation and Elimination in the Schools of Mauch Chunk Township. A. E. WAGNER.

———. Vol. III, No. 7. Dec. 1909:266. Size of Classes and School Progress. O. P. CORNMAN.

———.* Vol. III, No. 8. Jan. 1910:232; No. 9, Feb. 1910:255. Promotion, Retardation and Elimination. E. L. THORNDIKE.

———. Vol. IV, No. 1. Mar. 1910:1. What can and do School Reports show? R. P. FALKNER.

———. Vol. IV, No. 2. April 1910:46. Our Responsibility for Retardation. C. R. SQUIRE.

———. Vol. IV, No. 2. April 1910:40; No. 3, May 1910:79. Retardation and Elimination in Graded and Rural Schools. G. W. GAYLER.

———. Vol. IV, No. 4. June 1910:93. Medical and Dental Inspection in the Cleveland Schools. J. E. WALLIN.

———.* Vol. IV, No. 5. Oct. 1910:121. What is meant by Retardation? L. WITMER.

———. Vol. IV, No. 8. Jan. 1911:213. The Fundamental Expression of Retardation. R. P. FALKNER.

———. Vol. IV, No. 8. Jan. 1911:239. Age per Grade of Truant and Difficult School Boys. W. S. CORNELL.

———. Vol. V. No. 1. Mar. 1911:13. Retardation Statistics from the Smaller Minnesota Towns. F. E. LURTON.

*Special reference is made to this study.